Digital SLR Photography Demystified

by
Gordon H. Wood

www.filmscapes.ca

First Edition

First Printing: February 2014

All content (except cover) composed in Adobe® FrameMaker®
Front cover art composed in Adobe® Photoshop®

Cover design, illustration, text and photographs: Gordon H. Wood

First Edition

TABLE OF CONTENTS

Digital SLR Photography Demystified

LIST OF FIGURES

FOREWORD

Most of my students come to me for one-on-one still photography instruction because they've just purchased or received a digital single lens reflex camera (DSLR) and they're terrified to take the thing out of Auto mode. They know they can achieve better results but don't know how to go about doing so. In most cases, they find the camera's manual frustrating and nearly useless, or have watched numerous YouTube® videos but can't relate them to their own camera.

Indeed, much of my instruction time is spent helping them navigate the controls and menus on their specific camera to find the tools they need. While no one book can completely help with that, the intent in writing this one was to provide a reference guide for my current and past students as well as a starting point for anyone interested in self-instruction.

While the book title alludes to the reader who has no photographic experience whatsoever, I would hope the book also appeals to those who are already working with their DSLR but simply want to better understand photographic concepts and the camera's controls.

I believe that the only way a photographer becomes proficient is to practice, practice and practice again. That way, the relationship between aperture, shutter speed and ISO become old hat, and the photographer can then concentrate on getting the best results in a wide range of lighting scenarios. To that end, I have created photographic exercises throughout the book. Take the time to work through them without skipping steps, and you'll very likely have some 'a-ha' moments.

But don't throw away your camera's manual. Once you understand the concepts in this book, it should become easier to find out how to implement them in your camera using the manufacturer's manual to explain the controls and menus. You'll notice that I have kept icons and button functions fairly generic, but have shown more than one example in some cases to help you relate the topic to your specific camera model.

One final note on the purpose of this book. Although most late model DSLRs have excellent video-making capabilities, only *still* photography concepts are covered here.

Best of luck in your image-making!

Gordon

ABOUT THE AUTHOR

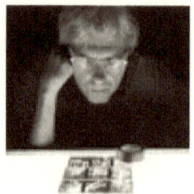

Trained as an engineer, Gordon Wood is a self-taught photographer. His images have appeared in international magazines, newspapers, books and brochures, and his photographic canvasses are currently appearing on walls throughout North America.

Starting out with 35mm film, he has also worked in medium and large for-mat film. Having fully embraced the digital imaging world, he now enjoys passing his knowledge on to eager students both at the college level and in one-to-one sessions.

Courses in digital photography, lighting and Photoshop® are taught in the London, Ontario, Canada area. Course listings and a free photography blog can be found at his website: **www.filmscapes.ca** (please note the *.ca* domain rather than .com)

ACKNOWLEDGEMENTS

I would like to thank Bill Conly and Simon Lee for proofreading my draft and providing valuable input.

AN INVITATION

If there is anything that stumps you in this book, or if you would like to provide feedback as to how to improve it, please feel free to email me at **questions@filmscapes.ca**. Include specific references to pages or topics, and I will be glad to address the issue for you.

CHAPTER 1: THE DSLR CAMERA TOUR

Introduction

Because every camera's arrangement of controls and buttons is unique, it would not be possible to identify the functions for every camera model in one book. If you can't immediately identify a control or menu item on your camera, use the specific topic in this chapter (eg. 'Command Wheel') to search your camera manual's index or the manufacturer's web site.

By presenting a generic camera representation in the following illustrations, though, the location of specific controls on your camera may be easier to find, since most camera controls are laid out in a similar fashion. Also, icons associated with each button or function are peppered throughout the book to assist you with your search. Keep in mind that these icons can vary considerably from camera to camera and are only representative of what may appear on your camera.

In the following pages, we'll take a tour of the DSLR and briefly describe the function of each of the most commonly-used controls and menu items. Don't worry if terminology comes up that you're not familiar with (like aperture, for instance) - these concepts will be described in detail in subsequent chapters. Once you've gained confidence in finding and understanding these functions, we'll move on to show you how to use them to take control of your images.

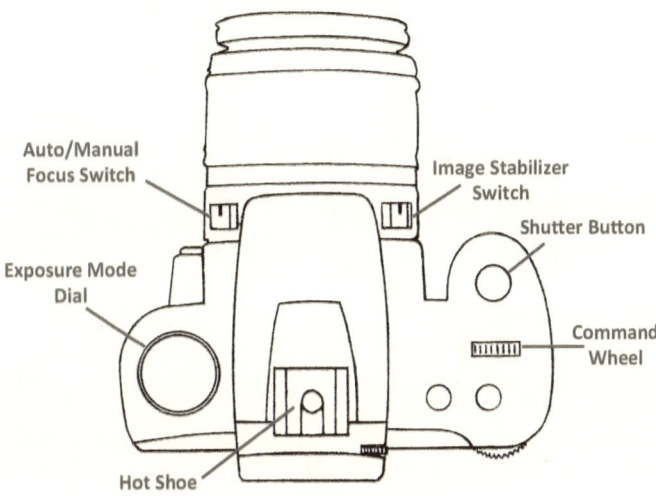

Figure 1 - 1 Generic DSLR Top View

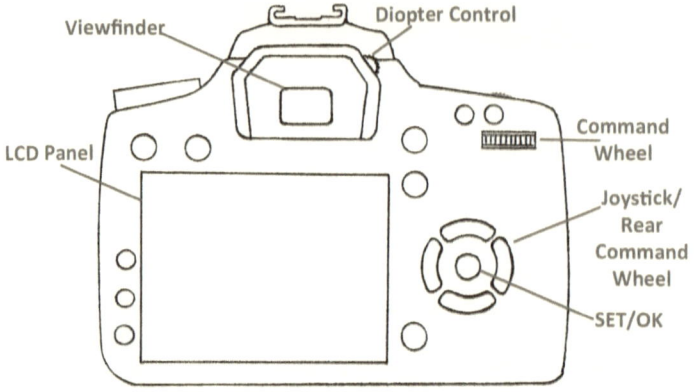

Figure 1 - 2 Generic DSLR Rear View

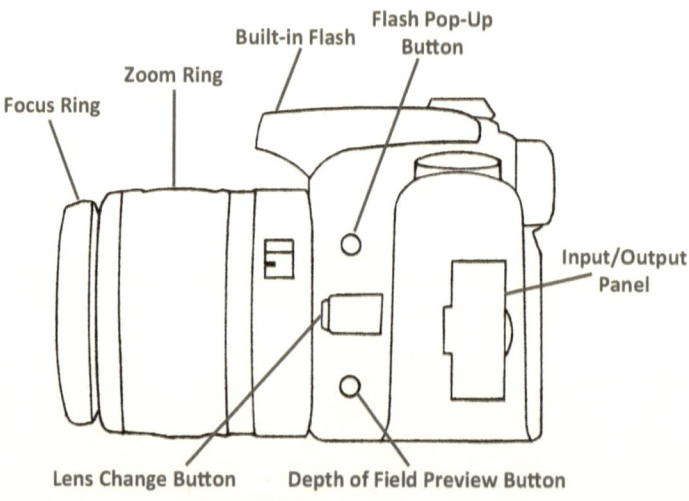

Figure 1 - 3 Generic DSLR Side View

Exposure Mode Dial

The method your camera uses to determine exposure is selected with this control. For this book, we are going to concentrate on the Creative Modes. These are comprised of:

- Program (P)
- Aperture Priority (Av or A)
- Shutter Priority (Tv or S)
- Manual (M)

 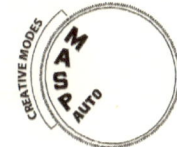

There are also a number of other special presets around the dial, but we are going to ignore those. Auto mode, however, will be briefly discussed.

Shutter Button

Pressing this button halfway will allow the camera to read the light and determine the exposure required. Pressing the button fully will result in the picture being taken.

Play Button

Your shots can be reviewed on the rear LCD panel once this button is pressed. You can scroll through the shots, usually by pressing the left and right side of the Joystick/Rear Command Wheel on the back of the camera.

Command Wheel(s)

Some cameras have a single Command Wheel on the front, near the shutter button, while others have a second one at the top rear of the camera. Their purpose is mainly to control aperture and shutter speed.

Joystick/Rear Command Wheel

Depending on the camera, this control has a number of functions, including scrolling through shots during playback and navigating menu items. In some cameras, it takes the place of the top rear Command Wheel mentioned above for control of aperture or shutter speed selection.

Menu Button

Access to camera settings that don't have a dedicated button on the outside of the camera is provided by the Menu button. The Joystick/Rear Command Wheel is typically used for navigation: pushing the top or bottom allows scrolling vertically through the Menu items, while pushing on the left or right let you see the choices within a Menu item. The SET or OK button in the middle of the Joystick/Rear Command Wheel is used to store your Menu selection in memory.

Special Function Buttons/Menu Items

Exposure Compensation

Depending on the camera model, this function is provided by a dedicated button, or by accessing a Menu item. Its purpose is to allow you to manually override the exposure determined by the camera's metering system and intentionally over- or underexpose the image by an amount selected by you.

Flash Exposure Compensation

This function is typically accessed through the camera's Menu button or through a shared button such as Exposure Compensation. It is different from Exposure Compensation in that it allows you to adjust only the flash output up or down without affecting the exposure determined by the camera. This can be used to control the pop-up flash, or, if attached to the hot shoe, a compatible accessory flash.

Auto Exposure Bracketing (AEB)

Often found in the same Menu group as Exposure Compensation and Flash Exposure Compensation, this function allows you to set up the camera to shoot three different exposures in a row: underexposed, normal and overexposed. The amount of under- or overexposure (in 'stops') is set by you in the Menu.

This is often used when in a tricky lighting situation where you're not sure if the camera is going to meter the light accurately. The other way it's used is for producing high dynamic range (HDR) images.

Turning off the camera usually turns off the AEB, but if you keep shooting without turning off the camera, AEB will still be active. Manually setting it to zero after use can be done in the Menu if you wish to continue shooting without AEB.

Info or Display

Pushing the Info button will display your camera's current settings, such as aperture, shutter speed and ISO, along with a host of other icons. Depending on the camera, pushing the Info button repeatedly when playing back your images will display the camera settings used to take each shot, as well as their histograms. On other cameras, pushing the up and down buttons on the rear joystick will provide this information during playback. Some cameras have a Display button instead, which functions like the Info button. These functions can vary widely between camera models, so it is advisable to research this topic in your camera's manual.

Live View

The Live View button flips up the camera's internal mirror to allow you to use the LCD panel instead of the optical viewfinder to frame up your shot. During this time, the viewfinder is dark. After taking the shot, the mirror returns to its normal position, making the viewfinder useable again. The most common use for Live View, however, is for shooting video. Warning - this function is hard on battery life.

White Balance

This function may be found as a dedicated button, or it may only be accessible through the Menu system. It consists of an Auto setting plus several presets. Its purpose is to ensure that colors are recorded accurately.

Auto white balance is typically used by default, but there are situations where a preset may be preferred. Typical examples are Daylight, Tungsten and Fluorescent. Custom white balance is also available to help you match a specific lighting setup.

ISO

In days of old when we shot on film, we would buy the film with a particular ISO rating. Essentially, the higher the ISO rating, the more sensitive to light the film was.

This is completely analogous to the ISO setting in digital cameras, in that the sensitivity is exactly the same as a film of the same ISO rating. The difference is that we can change ISO on-the-fly in the DSLR, whereas in film SLRs we had to wait for the film to be used completely before we could load another film with a different ISO rating.

ISO can be set to a specific value, such as 100 or 200, or you can leave it up to the camera to select the ISO in Auto mode.

Depth of Field Preview

This is a feature which sadly doesn't make it onto all DSLRs. A typical location for this button is shown in Figure 1 - 3. It allows you to assess the depth of field (the range of distance in front of the camera over which the image is in acceptable focus) when you select a particular aperture value (f/stop).

By pressing the shutter button halfway then pressing the Depth of Field button, you can preview in the viewfinder how much is going to be in focus at the aperture you've selected. The downside is that small apertures cut down the light considerably, making it sometimes difficult to determine the depth of field from a dark image. This is probably why some manufacturers don't bother with it, but it is a great device for helping you learn the relationship between depth of field and aperture without actually having to take a shot.

Metering Modes

Metering refers to the measurement, by the camera, of the amount of light coming through the lens. In all exposure modes except Manual (M), this allows the camera to automatically choose the settings required to produce a good exposure.

Evaluative/Matrix

Depending on camera brand, this mode is either called evaluative or matrix. Icons for both are shown at left. It means that the camera is measuring the light at several points in the scene and weighting them to produce a good average exposure. This is particularly helpful where the scene contains areas that differ greatly in light intensity, such as highlights and shadows.

Spot

While evaluative/matrix metering is very clever, there are scenarios where it may not produce desired results. If there is a subject in the scene that must be exposed properly (at the expense of the rest of the scene sometimes), spot metering can be employed to measure the light reflected specifically from the subject, and expose accordingly.

Spot metering does this by only measuring the light in 1 to 5% of the scene in the center of the viewfinder. Your camera's specifications should provide you with the specific percentage.

Partial

Similar to Spot metering, Partial typically measures the central 5 to 10% of the scene in the viewfinder. Some cameras provide Partial in place of Spot metering while others provide both.

Center Weighted

Taking the Spot/Partial metering concept one step further, Center Weighted metering measures the central 65 to 75% of the scene to determine the exposure. The icon varies depending on camera brand.

AF (Auto Focus) Modes

In Auto Focus, the camera's sensor system is looking for an edge or contrast in the scene that it can use to determine focus. It focuses by sending a signal to a dedicated focusing motor in the lens, which turns the focus ring until focus is achieved.

One Shot

In most cases, we will use the One Shot AF mode. By composing our scene in the viewfinder and pushing the shutter button halfway, the camera performs the focus function once. If the button is held, the focus point will be locked. That way, you can lock focus on a subject then recompose the shot as desired.

AI Servo

This mode is most suited to subjects that are constantly moving, such as children or athletes. While the shutter button is held down halfway, the lens will be continuously refocusing on the subject in motion.

AI Focus

If uncertain whether your subject will remain still or start moving (such as a pet), AI Focus will function in the same way as One Shot while they are stationary, but will switch to AI Servo automatically if the subject moves.

Auto Focus Area

You can choose to have Auto Focus work in a specific part of the scene or in all zones in the viewfinder. The latter is generally the default setting. This function is often accessed with a specific button, and the Command Wheel is used to select the focus zone or zones. The icon varies by camera brand.

If you have composed your shot in the viewfinder but the camera focuses on an object other than one you prefer, you might use this function to force the camera to focus on the preferred object by selecting a specific zone.

Of course, you can also switch the lens to Manual Focus (MF) and focus on the object manually.

Drive Mode

You can choose to either shoot only one picture each time the shutter is pushed (Single) or have the camera fire off several pictures in a row (Continuous) when the shutter is held down. Continuous mode is typically used when there is a lot of action in the scene. Drive mode may have a dedicated button on the camera body or may only be accessible through the Menu.

Flash Pop-Up Button

In the Creative Modes, the built-in flash will not deploy unless this button is pushed. When shooting inside or when fill flash is needed outdoors, you may choose to have the flash pop up.

Auto/Manual Focus Switch

This switch, found on the lens, either engages (Auto) or disengages (Manual) the auto focus function. When in Manual, the focus ring on the lens is disengaged from the focus motor, allowing you to turn the ring until your subject is in focus. The focus ring is often on the very front of the lens, but its position depends on the lens model.

Image Stabilizer Switch

Optical image stabilization is activated by this lens-mounted switch. This form of stabilization moves one of the internal lens elements with tiny motors to compensate for physical movement of the camera. This allows the use of slower shutter speeds, where shaking of the camera would normally cause a blurred image. Optical image stabilization is most beneficial at long focal lengths (telephoto) where camera movement gets magnified. It usually engages only when the shutter button is pressed halfway, to preserve battery life.

Some lenses have more than one setting available, each of which is tailored to a particular direction of motion (ie. horizontal or vertical).

Hot Shoe

Accessory Flash

If a more powerful flash than the one built into the camera is needed, a compatible accessory flash can be attached to the hot shoe. By selecting either TTL or ETTL mode on the flash, its light output will be controlled by the camera in the same way as the camera controls its built-in flash. Note that once an accessory flash is mounted on the hot shoe, the built-in flash will not pop up when the button is pressed.

<u>Remote Flash Trigger</u>

In situations where it is preferred to fire the accessory flash when not mounted on the camera's hot shoe, a remote trigger transmitter may be attached to the hot shoe instead. This radio transmitter activates a trigger receiver which fires the flash either through a hot shoe mounted on the receiver, or through a cable connecting the receiver and the flash.

Viewfinder/Diopter Control

The viewfinder is an optical means by which you can frame a shot. There is a mirror in the camera that reflects the image coming through the lens into a pentaprism. Because the lens projects a reversed image, the pentaprism rotates the image so that it is right-side-up and left-to-right in the viewfinder window. When you take the shot, the mirror momentarily flips up to allow the lens image to project onto the sensor.

Some people have 20/20 vision, whereas others need corrective lenses. In order to accommodate everyone's needs, camera manufacturers place a small diopter control thumbwheel next to the viewfinder to allow adjustment of its magnification. Turn the wheel for the sharpest image in the viewfinder.

Note that the viewfinder image is always provided at maximum aperture, unless you press the Depth of Field Preview button. In this way, you always are given the brightest image to help you frame and focus your shot before taking it.

Lens Change Button

Lenses are attached to the DSLR using a bayonet (turn and lock) mount. To unlock a lens and remove it from the camera, push and hold this button while turning the lens. At some point you will be able to lift the lens away from the camera body.

When mounting a lens to the body, align the dot on the lens with a similar mark on the body or mount, place it onto the mount and rotate the lens until a click is heard. At this point the lens is once again locked.

Input/Output Panel

Usually hidden behind a removable rubber flap are a number of jacks for accessory cables. These may include, but are not limited to, AV or HDMI for video, external microphone, remote shutter trigger and USB port.

CHAPTER 2: EXPOSURE

Our eyes and brain work together to allow us to see a tremendous range of light intensity from detail in the shadows to subtleties in bright highlights - all at the same time.

Unfortunately, what we see is not always what a DSLR sensor can capture. While the technology is amazing, modern sensors can only capture a limited brightness range. In fact, each color channel handles the information in 8 digital bits, meaning they can only resolve a maximum of 256 different levels of grey. This brightness range is referred to as dynamic range.

With a limited dynamic range, it's important to ensure we expose the sensor to the right level of brightness in order to capture the range of tones that are most important in our images. As we'll see in this chapter, the right exposure is determined by three main factors: aperture, shutter speed and ISO.

But first...some terminology explained.

Normal Exposure

As a loose definition, normal exposure means that the camera has satisfactorily captured everything we want in a picture from shadow to highlight detail, and everything in between.

Many scenes have a limited difference in light intensity between the brightest and darkest part of the scene (eg. a misty day). As a result, these fit within the dynamic range of the sensor. Some scenes that exceed the dynamic range of the sensor (eg. bright sunny scenes containing a lot of deep shadow detail) may still look acceptable with normal exposure because the slight loss of shadow and highlight detail may not comprise the majority of the scene.

Underexposure

Underexposure results from restricting the amount of light into the camera. Apart from the obvious disadvantage of having an overly dark image, the problem with underexposure is that we run the risk of not capturing all shadow detail in the camera. While we can often correct this in photo editing software, if the underexposure is extreme, no software can recover shadow detail that wasn't recorded in the first place. This is often referred to as 'crushing' the black information.

Overexposure

Severe overexposure results in loss of detail in the white areas of an image, commonly referred to as 'clipping' of the highlight information. As with underexposure, this detail is not always recoverable.

Both the under- and overexposure scenarios can be the result of the metering system in the camera getting fooled, or because the photographer chose the wrong settings when operating in Manual mode. More on this later.

The Histogram

The most important tool for evaluating exposure is the histogram. Typically, it is used in Play mode to determine if a recent shot was properly exposed, but it is often available in Live View to evaluate exposure settings before actually taking the picture.

The histogram is a statistical plot that shows how many pixels (the dots that make up the picture) are at each brightness ('grey scale') level in the picture. The height of the curve along the vertical axis represents the number of pixels at a particular brightness level and is plotted against the horizontal grey scale, which ranges from black at the left (0) end to white at the right (255) end. Mid-grey (often called 18% grey) is at 128. The numbers 0 to 255 represent the 256 shades of grey that the camera is capable of recording.

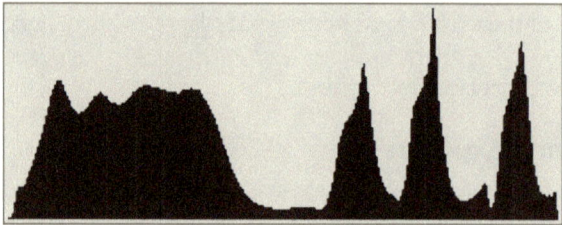

Figure 2 - 1 Histogram - Good Exposure

In Figure 2 - 1, for example, this histogram tells us that most of the information in the picture exists in the range between black and mid-grey. There are also three narrower peaks between mid-grey and full white, and these represent areas of the picture where there is grey, off-white and near-white information. This histogram tells us that the exposure in the picture it represents was good, because all the information is contained within the upper and lower limits of its horizontal scale.

So what does a histogram that represents a poorly exposed picture look like? Figure 2 - 2 shows a histogram from the scene in Figure 2 - 1, but now severely overexposed. Notice that the white information is rammed against the right hand edge and looks 'spikey'. Meanwhile, there are no pixels at the left edge of the histogram, which implies nothing is black in the picture. As you would expect, the picture looks washed out and detail in the highlights is 'clipped' or missing because it is outside of the maximum limit of the grey scale range that the camera can record. Similarly, under-exposure would give you a histogram rammed against the left edge instead, with little or no information at the right (white) edge.

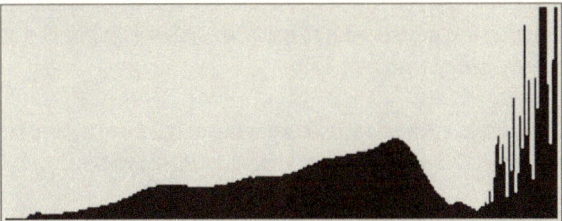

Figure 2 - 2 Histogram - Overexposure

The term grey scale does not imply that the camera can only record in black and white. Rather, it expresses the brightness level recorded in each of the sensor's three color channels: red, green and blue. When the information in these three channels is combined, of course, a color image is created.

In fact, you can also choose to display color histograms for each of the channels if you wish (Figure 2 - 3). The histograms in Figure 2 - 1 and Figure 2 - 2 are usually referred to as brightness histograms because they combine the red, green and blue channels into one.

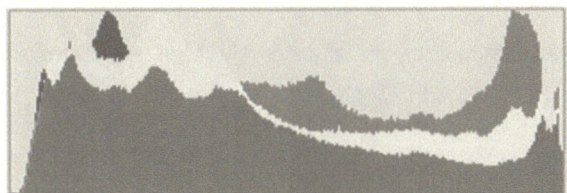

Figure 2 - 3 RGB Histogram

Aperture

Think of the iris in the eye. When we step into bright light outdoors, the brain tells the iris to restrict the amount of light entering the eye by forming a smaller opening. The opposite happens when we enter a dark room.

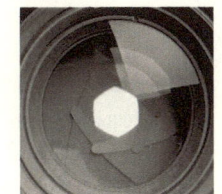

Figure 2 - 4 The Lens Aperture

This is exactly how the aperture operates within the camera lens. When the camera measures bright light in a scene, its computer 'brain' tells a set of blades in the lens to form a smaller opening (Figure 2 - 4). In this way, the aperture created by the blades is controlling the exposure within the camera.

The size of the opening is expressed numerically as an f/stop. The *higher* the f/number, the *smaller* the opening and the less light gets through. The lower the f/number, the more light passes into the camera. When the aperture blades are completely retracted, the *maximum* aperture that the lens can achieve is also expressed as an f/number. The lower the f/number at maximum aperture, the better the lens is at gathering light.

As an example, a lens with a maximum aperture of f/2.8 is considered superior to one rated at f/3.5 because the f/2.8 lens will perform better in low light situations.

Shutter Speed

While aperture controls the *amount* of light entering the camera, the shutter controls the *time* that the sensor is exposed to the light coming through the lens.

A good analogy for the action of the shutter mechanism is a cinema screen covered by curtains. We can't see the screen until one or both of the curtains are opened. In the camera's so-called focal plane shutter there are two curtains.

Initially, the curtains completely cover the sensor. When you take a picture by pressing the shutter button, the first curtain retracts completely, leaving the sensor completely exposed. After the shutter interval is complete (determined by the chosen shutter speed) the second curtain moves across to completely cover the sensor.

The shorter the shutter interval, the less light hits the sensor. Shorter intervals are chosen by setting the shutter speed to a smaller fraction of a second[1]. For example, 1/1000th of a second is a much shorter interval than 1/60th of a second. So, 1/1000th of a second shutter speed results in much less exposure than 1/60th of a second for the same amount of light coming through the lens.

Now a relationship between aperture and shutter speed becomes apparent. If a wide aperture (smaller f/number) is chosen, a shorter shutter interval (faster shutter speed) is required to maintain proper exposure. Conversely, choosing a smaller aperture (higher f/number) lets less light in, requiring the shutter to stay open longer (slower shutter speed) for the same exposure.

Let's look at an example. If your camera meters the scene and determines that aperture should be set to f/8 and a shutter speed of 1/500th of a second, if you chose f/11 instead, the camera would have to reset the shutter speed to 1/250th of a second in order to provide the exact same exposure. Photographers often refer to this as closing the aperture by one stop[2] and slowing the shutter speed by one stop. One stop means halving or doubling the exposure. In this example, we halved

---

1. Note that shutter speed can also be set to 1 second or greater, resulting in even more exposure than fractional second speeds.
2. The term 'stop' is loosely used when referring to the relative change of either aperture or shutter speed by a factor of two, whereas 'f/stop' is an absolute number that refers to the specific aperture value (eg. f/5.6).

the light coming into the camera by one stop with aperture but doubled the time the sensor was exposed to the light.

Shutter speeds can either be fractions of a second or one second and longer. On your camera's LCD panel or in its viewfinder, fractional seconds are usually shown as a whole number. For example, 1/125th of a second is shown as 125. One second or slower speeds are shown with a double quotation mark after the number. So, one second is shown as 1", two and a half seconds is shown as 2"5 and thirty seconds is shown as 30". There are some exceptions - larger fractions of one second are not always shown as a whole number: one half second may be displayed as 0"5 instead of 2.

ISO

As explained in Chapter 1, ISO represents the sensitivity of the sensor. Every time the ISO value is changed by a factor of two, the sensitivity is doubled or halved. Such changes have the same effect as changing the aperture or shutter speed by one stop.

To use our previous example, let's assume that the ISO in our camera is set to 200 and the camera has determined that f/8 and 1/500th of a second are required for a good exposure. If we set the ISO to 100 and meter the same scene, the camera will now require the settings to be changed to either f/8 and 1/250th of a second or f/5.6 (one stop wider aperture than f/8) and 1/500th of a second. That's because we have halved the sensitivity of the sensor so we need to increase the exposure by one stop to compensate. The one stop exposure increase can either be implemented by opening the aperture by one whole f/stop (without changing the shutter speed) or by keeping the shutter open twice as long (without changing the aperture).

We can now see how the relationship between aperture, shutter speed and ISO emerges. All three are the prime factors that affect exposure, because changing any one by one stop requires that one of the remaining two must be changed by one stop to maintain the same exposure.

With most DSLRs you have the choice of letting the camera set the ISO automatically (Auto) or setting it to a specific value. In Auto ISO mode, the camera will choose as high an ISO value as necessary to allow you to use a reasonably fast shutter speed. This is because slow shutter speeds usually result in blur due to camera or subject motion. In low light situations, a high ISO will help with this situation.

Of course, there is a limit to everything. In the case of ISO, as it is increased, more and more 'noise' is introduced into the picture. This may present as graininess or spots that weren't in the original scene.

The disadvantage of using Auto ISO is that you may not be aware that the camera has chosen a very high setting that results in noise. If instead you manually set the ISO to a value that provides a noiseless image, you could intentionally slow the shutter speed down or open the aperture more to compensate for the lower sensitivity. How you do this is the subject of the following sections.

STARTING TIP: Set ISO to 200 for most shooting. Feel free to use a higher setting in low light, particularly if you can't use flash. Higher ISO will allow faster shutter speeds, so you can capture the shot without the blur associated with slow shutter speeds. Remember, though, that higher ISO=more noise.

Exposure Modes

As we discovered in Chapter 1, the Exposure Mode dial lets us choose how we want to control our exposure settings. In the graphic shown here, the Creative Modes are labelled differently depending on camera model. While we will be concentrating on the Creative Modes for the remainder of this book, we'll first briefly touch on the Auto Mode.

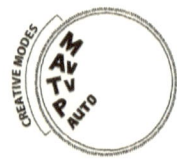 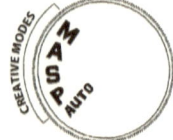

Auto

When you first took your camera out of the box, chances are the Exposure Mode dial was set to Auto by the factory. This is because most people unfamiliar with the DSLR just want to start taking good pictures right away without reading a manual.

For the most part, Auto mode covers this off very well. To take better pictures, though, Auto mode falls short because it takes away control of *how* you take the picture.

In Auto mode, when you press the shutter button, a number of parameters are determined for you. These are: aperture, shutter speed, ISO and flash. The problem is that if you don't like the settings it chooses, or you don't want the built-in flash to fire, you have no say in the matter.

Why does it matter what the settings are? As you will see in later chapters on Depth of Field and The Shutter, there are particular circumstances where you will need to take control of aperture and shutter speed to get the results you want. Hence the Creative Modes.

Creative Modes

Program (P) and Program Shift

This mode is as close as you're going to get to Auto, but this time you get some control.

When you press the shutter button halfway, the camera provides you with a combination of aperture and shutter speed. ISO, however, remains at whatever value you last set it to, unless you left it in Auto ISO. Further, the built-in flash will not pop up and fire unless you push its 'lightning bolt' button.

If you don't like the aperture and shutter speed it has chosen, you can use Program Shift to change the combination. Why? You may want to use a faster shutter speed than the camera has chosen because you want to capture a fast-moving subject, or you may want to

---

choose a higher f/stop (smaller aperture) to obtain greater depth of field (more on this later).

So, Program mode gives you a starting point, but Program Shift lets you tweak it. In most cameras, Program Shift is provided by the Command Wheel, but you may need to refer to the manual to verify this. Simply press the shutter button halfway to get the initial settings, then rotate the Command Wheel to change the aperture/shutter speed combination.

Aperture Priority (Av or A)

If controlling the aperture is important (for reasons that will be explained later), a particular f/stop value may be chosen in this mode by turning the Command Wheel. You should be able to see this choice change on the LCD panel as you turn the Command Wheel.

Aperture Priority mode implies that the user selects the aperture and the camera selects the shutter speed that will give a proper exposure. This is based on the light that the camera reads coming through the lens. The aperture value will never change until you change it, but the shutter speed will change as the light in the scene changes. In this sense it is a semi-automatic mode.

Shutter Priority (Tv or S)

Similarly, Shutter Priority is also a semi-automatic mode. The user selects the shutter speed they want to use and the camera sets the aperture based on the light it reads.

Manual (M)

Manual mode hearkens to the days of old when everything on mechanical film cameras had to be set manually. There is no automation involved because the camera doesn't actually set either the aperture or shutter speed. These must be set individually by the user.

What the camera does for you in this mode is to provide an exposure indication in the form of a bar graph. One variation is shown below, but the style may differ with camera model. If the bar graph indicator moves either side of the central zero point, you adjust either aperture or shutter speed to zero it again. Once zeroed, the exposure should be good. Professionals typically use a separate handheld meter to do the same thing.

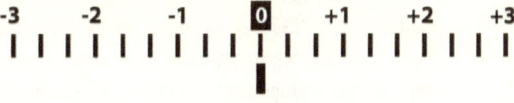

The means by which you adjust aperture and shutter speed separately varies with camera model. If there is only one Command Wheel, shutter speed is usually controlled by it. To set the aperture, usually you push and hold the Exposure Compensation button while turning the Command Wheel. Some cameras have two Command Wheels, in which case one is dedicated to aperture while the other is dedicated to shutter speed. In some models, the second Command Wheel is the Joystick/Command Wheel on the back panel of the camera.

In case you're wondering why you would want to bother with Manual mode, many professionals need it for studio lighting shots. As we'll also see later, it also provides more options for those interested in time exposures and panoramic photography.

The Camera's Light Meter

Reflected Light

You will often see the acronym TTL used when referring to the method that the camera uses to determine the required exposure. This stands for **T**hrough **T**he **L**ens, which implies that the camera measures the light that is gathered by the lens. This light is that which is reflected from the scene, rather than the light falling on it (ie. *incident* light).

The Meaning of 18% Grey

In the earlier discussion on histograms, the concept of 18% grey was introduced. This level of grey sits right in the middle of the histogram's horizontal scale, halfway between the darkest black that the camera can record to the brightest white detail.

The concept of 18% grey has been used by photographers long before digital photography and histograms. By reading the light reflected off a surface that has been calibrated to 18% grey, such as a grey card (available from camera stores), the camera's exposure setting can be more accurately set than by relying on the light reflected from the scene. In this way, it is measuring incident rather than reflected light.

If you can find an 18% grey card, here's an exercise you can try with your DSLR. Go outside, set your exposure mode to Program and fill the camera's viewfinder with the light evenly reflected from the card. Take a shot and review it with the Play button. Now, look at the histogram for that shot. If the card was evenly illuminated by daylight, you should see a single 'spike' sitting right at the middle of the histogram. If so, it means your metering system is accurate. If it's significantly above the middle, your camera tends to overexpose. It is underexposing if it falls significantly below the middle.

Evaluative or Matrix Metering

So why should we care about 18% grey?

Every metering method used by the camera sets the exposure based on *averaging* the reflected light reading to 18% grey. The reason for this is that the camera is attempting to expose the image such that its histogram will be centered around the middle of its horizontal scale. In doing so, it is attempting to ensure that no shadow or highlight detail gets lost by having one end of the histogram or the other rammed against the left or right end of the horizontal scale.

Evaluative (Canon) or Matrix (Nikon) metering modes take the 18% grey concept one step further. If a scene contains both bright highlight and dark shadow detail, a single metering area may favour either a highlight or a shadow area, depending on how the scene is framed. This will possibly result in either an underexposed or overexposed image because the metering system is telling the camera to expose for an average 18% grey for the metered area.

If you were now to meter over several points in the scene, and apply weighting to each of those points depending upon how many were at the same or similar light intensity, you would obtain a better average exposure. Evaluative and Matrix metering both employ several sensors and calculate an average which is used to set the camera's exposure to create an image with an average content of 18% grey. This is called Evaluative Through The Lens metering, or ETTL.

Spot or Partial Metering

In strongly backlit scenes (eg. a person against a window but facing the camera), Evaluative/ Matrix metering can result in facial features that become too dark. This is because the majority of the scene is extremely bright, and the metering attempts to average the backlight to approximately 18% grey. The result is underexposure.

Spot and Partial metering work around this problem by metering the light only at the center of the viewfinder.

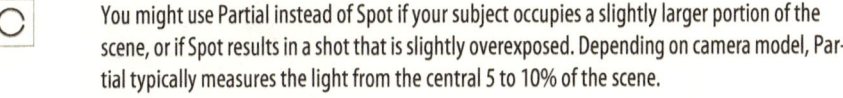

Spot metering measures the light at the central 1 to 5% (camera-dependent) of the scene in the viewfinder. By centering your subject in the viewfinder, the light reflected from the subject rather than the backlight will determine the exposure.

You might use Partial instead of Spot if your subject occupies a slightly larger portion of the scene, or if Spot results in a shot that is slightly overexposed. Depending on camera model, Partial typically measures the light from the central 5 to 10% of the scene.

Center Weighted Metering

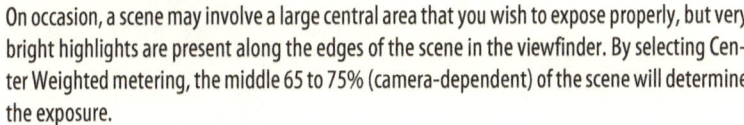

On occasion, a scene may involve a large central area that you wish to expose properly, but very bright highlights are present along the edges of the scene in the viewfinder. By selecting Center Weighted metering, the middle 65 to 75% (camera-dependent) of the scene will determine the exposure.

This is a metering mode I rarely if ever use, because Evaluative/Matrix metering generally works well under this condition. As a historical note, Center Weighted metering emulates the metering found in older manual film cameras.

Fooling the Camera's Light Meter

Reflected light meters do not always accurately measure the overall light intensity if the scene has either extreme variation in content or a predominantly bright or dark area.

Take the example of a snow covered field and an overcast sky. If the snow comprises most of the scene, evaluative or matrix metering will create an image with grey-looking snow. Why? Remember that metering systems always attempt to set the exposure so that the content in the scene averages 18% grey. If bright white snow fills the frame, the metering system wants to force it to the middle of the histogram. Similarly, taking a picture inside a dark cave will result in an image with grey walls rather than black.

Even scenes with both bright highlights and dark shadow areas can result in wrong exposure. If highlights, for example, comprise the majority of the scene, most of the light measurement zones will use the highlights to determine exposure. When evaluative or matrix metering determines an average, it will weight the highlight zones higher than the shadow areas in this case. The result is highlights that are more grey than white, and possibly loss of very dark shadow detail. The histogram would show that most of the content has slid toward the lower edge rather than being centered (Figure 2 - 5).

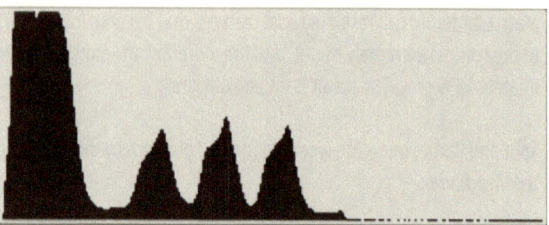

Figure 2 - 5 Histogram - Underexposure

Exposure Compensation

One workaround for the situation where the camera's meter gets fooled is to use Spot or Partial metering and aim the camera at an object that is mid-grey. By holding the shutter button down halfway, this exposure setting will now be locked until you recompose the scene in the viewfinder (if desired) and take the shot.

 If that method seems too difficult, you can use Exposure Compensation instead. The method varies depending on camera model, but if your camera has the button shown at left, press and hold it while rotating the Command Wheel. If the shot you previously took was underexposed, dial in positive compensation. If overexposed, dial in negative compensation. The amount is up to you, but in snow scenes, I typically use up to +2 stops.

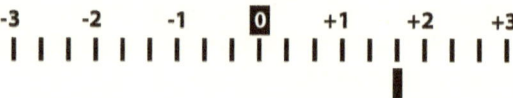

Photographic Exercise 1

This exercise will give you practice with the histogram so that you will understand how to use it to ensure proper exposure.

1. Take a picture using any exposure mode you wish, but you may find it easiest to start with Program (P) mode.
2. Press the Play button to show the image on the camera's LCD panel.
3. Press the Info button repeatedly (varies between cameras – check your manual to determine how to display histograms) until you see the histogram. If it is comprised of three graphs (red, green and blue), go into the menu system, look for Histogram, and if you can find it, change it from RGB to Brightness. This will give you a single histogram that represents the red, green and blue channels combined. If you can't find it, RGB will do.
4. Analyze the histogram. Does it look fairly balanced toward the middle, or is it skewed to the left or the right? A centered histogram that tapers off gradually at both ends is properly exposed. One that is skewed heavily to the left is underexposed and may have lost shadow detail. One that is skewed heavily to the right is overexposed and may have lost highlight detail.
5. Take the same shot, but this time dial in 2 stops of overexposure (+) beforehand using the Exposure Compensation button and the Command Wheel (this method will vary from camera to camera – check your manual under Exposure Compensation). On the camera's LCD panel, you will see a metering scale that should show the exposure compensation you have set, when you press the shutter button halfway. Use the Play button to review the image and its histogram. If it was properly exposed before, it will now be overexposed with a (possibly spikey-looking) histogram that is skewed badly to the right. If the first shot was underexposed, you can see how using Exposure Compensation and taking a second shot will result in a more balanced or centered histogram, depending on how much compensation you use.
6. Repeat 5. using 2 stops of underexposure (-).
7. With the 2 stops of underexposure still dialed in, turn off the camera, wait a few seconds, and switch it on again. Check the camera's meter scale. Has it returned to zero when you press the shutter button halfway? Probably not. This means that you must remember to set Exposure Compensation to zero when you no longer need it or your next shot will be under- or overexposed.

Photographic Exercise 2

In this exercise, we'll work with a couple of metering modes to see which works best in a specific lighting scenario. You can use Program, Aperture Priority or Shutter Priority modes for this exercise – your choice. Do not use Manual mode.

1. Set up a scenario where the subject (preferably a person) is strongly backlit. An example of this would be to make them stand against a brightly lit window but facing in to the room. Do not place them near a reflecting wall or a lamp. The goal is to make their face dark relative to the window light.

2. Take a shot of them against the window. Keep the focal length short enough to mostly fill the shot with window light. By default, your camera's metering is probably set to Evaluative (Canon) or Matrix (Nikon) at this point.

3. Use the metering button if your camera has one, or use the menu to change the metering method to Spot or Partial metering. Center the subject's face in the viewfinder and take another shot. Make sure your lens is set at the same focal length as the previous shot.

Analysis:

In the first shot, the camera was measuring the light at several points in the scene using Evaluative or Matrix metering. As part of its exposure calculation, it took into account the bright window light as a large part of the scene. Since the camera's metering system averages the light it reads over several places in the scene to produce an overall 18% grey exposure, it is heavily influenced by the bright window light, and tries to make it close to 18% grey. The result is an underexposed picture with a grey window light and the subject's face very dark.

In the second shot, the Spot metering is only measuring light at the center of the scene. If you centered the subject's face properly in the viewfinder, it will set the exposure such that the subject's face is now 18% grey (in brightness). The window light will be very bright, and any detail will be blown out (check the histogram to confirm this). Your subject is now properly exposed. Note that you could have left the metering in Evaluative or Matrix mode and used Exposure Compensation to achieve the same result, but then you would have to experiment to see how much compensation was needed. Spot metering, however, lets the camera determine that for you.

Now remember to reset your metering mode to Evaluative or Matrix mode or you'll get some wonky results in your subsequent photos!

CHAPTER 3: DEPTH OF FIELD

Definition

One very important photographic concept that needs to be understood in order to take complete control of your results is depth of field. Simply stated, it is the range in front of the camera over which your photograph will be in acceptable focus.

If we are taking landscape photographs, it is usually desireable to have everything in focus from just in front of the camera out to the horizon. This requires a large (or deep) depth of field.

Portrait photographers, on the other hand, try to have the background and foreground out of focus but most if not all of their subject in focus (particularly the eyes). A short (or shallow) depth of field provides this effect.

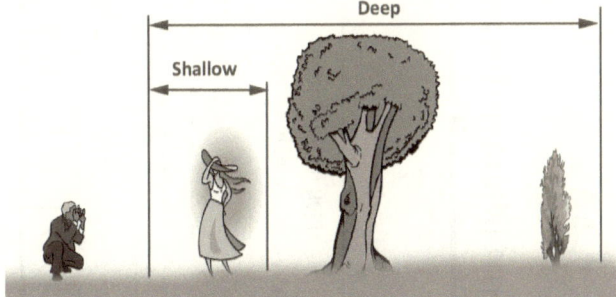

Figure 3 - 1 The Concept of Depth of Field

The f/stop Chart

In Chapter 2, the concept of aperture and f/stops was introduced. Here, we will learn why the choice of aperture is important. In short, there is a direct relationship between aperture (in f/stops) and depth of field (in feet or meters): *the smaller the aperture (or the higher the f/stop number), the greater the depth of field.*

Table 1 shows this relationship. Note that the f/stops shown across the top of the chart are full f/stops apart. That is, if we changed aperture from f/2.8 to f/4 in Aperture Priority mode (Av or A), for example, we are now letting half the amount of light through the lens. This would require the shutter speed to be changed to half the speed (open twice as long) that it was at f/2.8 in order to maintain the same exposure.

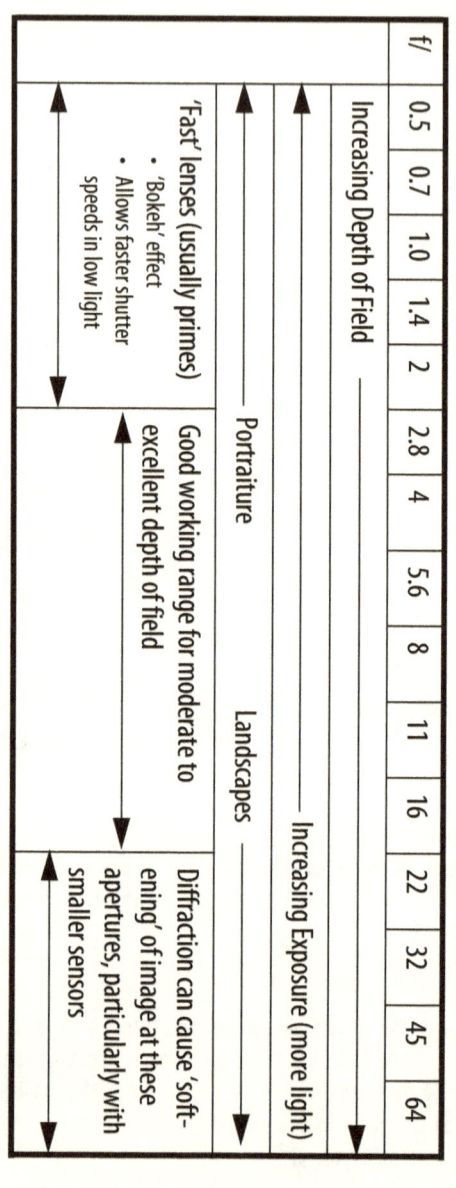

Table 1 Effect of Aperture on Depth of Field and Exposure

f/	0.5	0.7	1.0	1.4	2	2.8	4	5.6	8	11	16	22	32	45	64

Increasing Depth of Field →

Increasing Exposure (more light) →

Portraiture

Landscapes

'Fast' lenses (usually primes)
- 'Bokeh' effect
- Allows faster shutter speeds in low light

Good working range for moderate to excellent depth of field

Diffraction can cause 'soft-ening' of image at these apertures, particularly with smaller sensors

Of course, there are other aperture values that don't appear in the chart (eg. f/3.5). These would be considered fractional stops in relation to the values shown in the chart. The difference between f/3.5 and f/5.0, for example, is also one full stop, but they are each one third of a stop wider in aperture than f/4 and f/5.6, respectively.

The chart also expresses the relationship between f/stop and the amount of light passing through the lens. Again, a smaller f/number means a physically wider aperture is formed, allowing more light into the camera. So, opening the aperture wider means that you can use a faster shutter speed, but depth of field will be reduced. This is why 'faster' lenses, capable of smaller f/numbers at maximum aperture, are preferred by portrait photographers who are trying to achieve very shallow depth of field.

Most 'fast' lenses are prime lenses, which will be discussed in the next chapter. One benefit of ultra wide apertures is an effect called *bokeh*. This is a Japanese word that refers to the large petal-like points of light created when photographing with background light sources that are beyond the depth of field range and are therefore extremely out of focus. Your subject in this scenario will be in the foreground and within the depth of field range, and therefore in focus. The result is extreme separation between subject and background, with the background taking on a surreal look.

As the chart implies, it is not recommended that apertures smaller than f/22 be used, particularly on APS-C and smaller sensors (more on sensor sizes in the next chapter). At these apertures, bending of the light (diffraction) is more pronounced around the edge of the aperture blades, causing a slight de-focus effect. This would be noticeable when printing enlargements, but not so on snapshot prints. Diffraction effect is less evident on larger sensors or film. For example, apertures in the order of f/64 can be used without concern on large format film cameras that produce huge 4"x5" negatives.

Depth of Field Examples

If your camera has a depth of field preview button (described in Chapter 1), you can dial in a particular aperture using aperture priority mode (Av or A) with your Command Wheel and see how deep or shallow your depth of field will be. If you don't have this feature, you can always load a depth of field calculator on your smartphone, or refer to web sites like dofmaster.com.

To get a sense of how depth of field is affected by aperture, here are a few examples. You can try these using your smartphone app or the Depth of Field Calculator on dofmaster.com:

- Using a Canon camera with an APS-C sensor, if we are taking a portrait of someone 3 feet away using a 55mm focal length lens set to an aperture of f/2, we will have a very shallow depth of field of 0.06 feet. If we focused on our subject's eyes at exactly 3 feet, then anything closer than 2.97 feet or further than 3.03 feet will be out of acceptable focus.
- Using that same Canon camera and 55mm lens focused on the subject at 3 feet, setting the aperture to f/22 instead will result in everything being in acceptable focus from about 2.7 feet from the camera to about 3.4 feet from the camera. Depth of field has increased from 0.06 to 0.7 feet by changing only the aperture from f/2 to f/22. According to Table 1, this is equivalent to 7 stops of aperture change.

- Using a Nikon camera with a full frame sensor and again a 55mm lens set to f/22, and focusing on a subject at 6 feet, the depth of field is now about 5.7 feet. Anything in the range of about 4.3 feet to 10 feet from the camera will be in acceptable focus.
- As will be discussed in the chapter on Lenses and Sensors, focal length also affects depth of field. Using that same Nikon camera, if we now switched to a 35mm focal length lens, set aperture to f/22 and focused again on our subject at 6 feet, our depth of field now covers about 3 feet to more than 1000 feet from the camera. Quite a dramatic difference!

At first glance, it may appear that the smaller sensor on the Canon camera yields only very shallow depth of field compared to the full frame Nikon. While the larger sensor does provide a somewhat deeper depth of field for the same focal length and aperture, subject distance also comes into play. For instance, with the Canon APS-C camera and 55mm lens, using f/22 but this time focusing on a subject at 10 feet instead of 3 feet, depth of field now increases from 0.7 feet to 10.4 feet (7 feet to 17.4 feet in focus).

> **STARTING TIP:** If you are shooting family portraits and want a soft background, use aperture priority mode and set an aperture of f/8 or wider (eg. f/3.5). If shooting landscapes, start with an aperture between f/16 and f/22, if there is enough light in the scene.

Shifting the Depth of Field with Focus (Hyperfocal Distance)

We just touched on the effect of focus distance on the *extent* of the depth of field. Think about what also happens when you focus at greater and greater distances from the camera: the depth of field range itself also *moves* further from the camera. An example is shown in Figure 3 - 2.

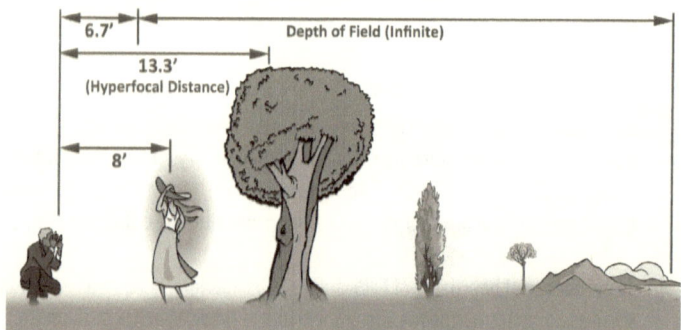

Figure 3 - 2 Hyperfocal Distance

Once again, we'll use the Canon APS-C camera, but this time with a 35mm focal length lens. Aperture is set to f/16 in Figure 3 - 2. If our subject is at 8 feet, focusing on the subject would result in a depth of field that only ranges from 5 feet to 14.8 feet. (You can verify this with dofmaster.com).

If we now wanted to keep our subject in focus, but also wanted to keep everything behind our subject in focus out to the horizon, we would have to focus *beyond* our subject. This new focus distance is called *hyperfocal distance*. In this example, we simply need to focus at 13.3 feet instead of 8 feet to achieve a depth of field ranging from 6.7 feet out to infinity. Our subject at 8 feet away is still in focus, but so is the horizon.

This technique is of particular interest to landscape or architectural photographers. It's not one you can do on the fly, because most lenses for digital cameras don't have a distance scale, so you would have to measure out the hyperfocal distance in some way. Note that this technique also requires you to *manually* focus, since autofocus would likely focus on the subject at 8 feet. And, to figure out what the hyperfocal distance has to be in the first place, you'll either need to print out a table or get that smartphone app.

Photographic Exercise 3

This exercise demonstrates how depth of field and aperture are related.
1.	If using a zoom lens, set its focal length to about 35mm. If using a prime (fixed focal length) lens, whatever the focal length of the lens is will be fine. Leave the focal length the same throughout the exercise. Set the AF/MF switch on the lens to MF (manual focus)
2.	Set the Exposure Mode dial to Aperture Priority (Av or A) and set aperture to f/5.6 using the Command Wheel.
3.	Place an object under bright light at about 2 feet from the camera & another at about 6 feet from the camera & take a shot (manually focus on the object at 2 feet using the focus ring – again, don't change the focal length on the zoom lens).
4.	Change aperture to f/16 & take the same shot (or push the Depth of Field Preview button while looking through the viewfinder). How does the focus change on the background object?

Analysis of results:
You should notice that at f/16, the object at 6 feet is sharper than at f/5.6. Remember that the focus was fixed on the object at 2 feet (because you manually focused, right?), so the increased depth of field provided by an aperture of f/16 brought the object at 6 feet more into focus.

NOTES:

CHAPTER 4: THE SHUTTER

The shutter determines the amount of time that the sensor is exposed to the light coming from the lens. The primary mode we can use to set shutter speed is Shutter Priority, but as we saw in Chapter 2 (Exposure), Manual (M) and Program (P - using Program Shift) can also be used to control it.

Shutter Priority Mode (Tv or S)

In Chapter 3 (Depth of Field), we learned that by using Aperture Priority (Av or A) mode, we took control over how much of our image was in focus. Based on the amount of light in the scene, the camera automatically chose a shutter speed for us, while keeping the aperture where we set it.

Shutter Priority works in reverse. We choose what shutter speed we want to use and the camera now automatically chooses an aperture to give us the right exposure. The shutter speed will remain the same until we either change it with the Command Wheel or leave Shutter Priority mode altogether. Of course, the consequence of letting the camera choose the aperture is that we no longer have complete control over depth of field.

There are times, however, when shutter speed is more important than depth of field. If you're a sports photographer, you may choose a fast shutter speed to freeze action. Landscape photographers on the other hand may wish to use very slow shutter speeds to intentionally blur movement in a waterfall or clouds.

Keep in mind that if you set a fast shutter speed, the aperture that the camera automatically chooses in Shutter Priority mode may not give you sufficient depth of field for the shot you want. The aperture choice is completely dependent on the amount of light that the camera reads and the ISO setting, so if you want more depth of field (a higher f/number), you can always set a higher ISO value in the camera.

Fast Shutter Speeds

We use fast shutter speeds to capture fast moving objects without blur. Blur is caused when the shutter stays open for a sufficient amount of time to allow our subject to change position within the frame. Their motion is recorded on the sensor as a trail while they move.

Figure 4 - 1 shows an example shot at approximately 1/1000th of a second. This would appear as 1000 on our LCD panel or in the viewfinder. That sort of speed was required to make the water droplets appear sharp. At slower shutter speeds (1/500th of a second or slower), the droplets would have started to show a motion trail. Of course, a strong light source was required to allow such a fast shutter speed to be used.

Note that the depth of field is somewhat shallow, because the camera had to choose a wide aperture (small f/number) in order to ensure proper exposure. If there was not enough light to take the shot, the aperture value would flash on and off on the LCD panel or in the viewfinder, indicating that the lens cannot open wide enough to expose the image properly. Some cameras show the phrase 'Low Light' in the LCD panel. In this case, you could either dial in a higher ISO value (preferred for this shot) or select a slower shutter speed.

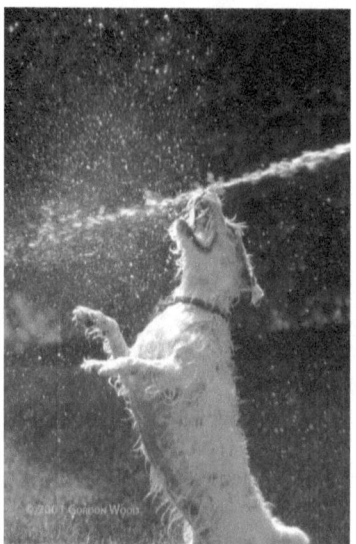

Figure 4 - 1 Fast Shutter Example

Slow Shutter Speeds

The river scene in Figure 4 - 2 was shot using a relatively long time exposure of about one second. This would show in the LCD panel or viewfinder display as 1". In this case, we want the water motion to create a blur so that it assumes a creamy, surreal look. Forcing such a slow shutter speed has the benefit of allowing a very small aperture (large f/number) to be used, thereby giving us greater depth of field.

By setting a moderate shutter speed (1/60th or 1/30th of a second) we obtain the result in Figure 4 - 3. This takes a lot of practice to get right, but by panning horizontally with our fast-moving subject, the background becomes blurred but the subject stays reasonably sharp.

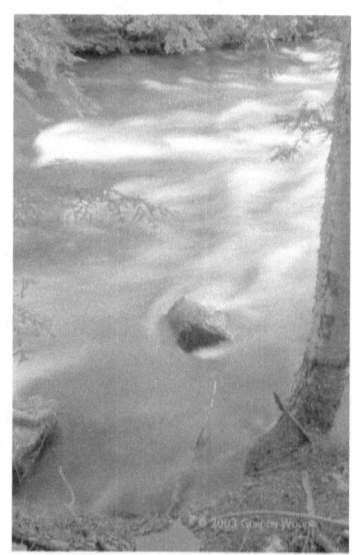

Figure 4 - 2 Slow Shutter Example

The subject is now separated from the background and there is an implied sense of motion from the streaking background.

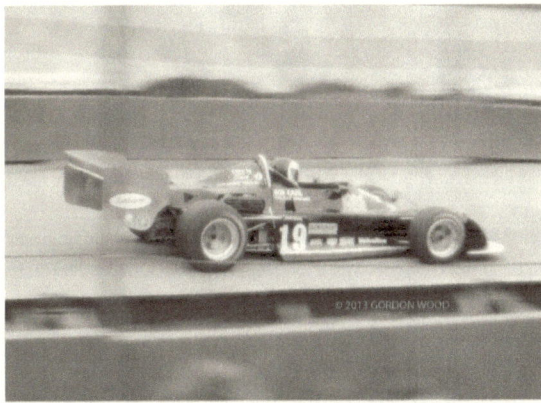

Figure 4 - 3 Panning Motion Example

Flash Sync Speeds

Back in Chapter 2 (Exposure), the dual curtain shutter mechanism was described. When the shutter button is pressed fully, the first curtain exposes the sensor completely, then the second curtain covers it up after the first curtain has completely retracted.

As higher and higher shutter speeds are selected, eventually the two curtains must form a narrower and narrower moving slit in order to reduce the amount of time that the sensor is exposed. In other words, at these speeds, there is never a time when the entire sensor is exposed because the second curtain is now starting to cover the sensor before the first curtain has completely revealed it.

The light from the flash is a very short burst that is typically much faster than the most commonly used shutter speeds. The flash and shutter are synchronized so that the flash only fires when the sensor is completely exposed. That way, the reflected light from the flash completely illuminates the sensor.

But what happens when the selected shutter speed is so high that the curtains are now forming a slit instead of exposing the entire sensor? Because the flash duration is much shorter than most shutter speeds, the reflected light from the flash now only illuminates the part of the sensor visible through the slit. The shutter speed at which this starts to occur is faster than the Flash Sync speed, which is typically about 1/200th of a second (camera-dependent). This means that you won't be able to use blazing speeds like 1/1000th of a second to freeze motion while using the flash.

Manufacturers get around this problem by making some camera models compatible with accessory flashes capable of high speed sync mode. This mode is often designated FP (Focal Plane) or

HSS (High Speed Sync), which fires the flash several times during exposure. This allows it to illuminate the sensor entirely as the slit crosses the sensor. The downside is that flash output drops in FP mode, requiring a very wide aperture on a fast lens to ensure proper exposure at very high shutter speeds.

First and Second Curtain Sync

The camera's menu system will often allow you to determine when the flash fires by choosing either first or second curtain synchronization.

Assume you are taking a long exposure at night with a car approaching you. Exposure times may be in the order of one second or longer in such a shot, depending on the light in the scene.

If you choose first curtain synchronization, the flash will fire immediately after the first curtain has completely retracted (at the beginning of the exposure). The car will be illuminated by the flash when it is furthest from you. For the remainder of the exposure, the headlights will create streaks that appear ahead of the car because the car is now getting closer to you.

With second curtain synchronization, the opposite occurs. The flash fires at the *end* of the exposure when the car is closest to you. Prior to that, the headlights produce streaks during the long exposure. The result is that the streaks appear behind the car because they were formed before the flash fired and exposed the car.

Photographic Exercise 4

Let's put some of what you've learned about the camera and exposure to work. This exercise demonstrates how aperture, shutter speed and ISO work together to produce a properly exposed image. Read through the instructions completely before beginning and take your time to understand the results.

1. If using a zoom lens, set its focal length to about 35mm (or using a fixed focal length lens of any other focal length will do). If you have a tripod or solid surface to place the camera on, please use it for this exercise. Aim the camera at a scene or object and leave it there. Do not change the focal length throughout this exercise.
2. Push the ISO button or go into the camera's menu and find the ISO setting. Ensure that ISO is *not* set to Auto. If it is, set it to a fixed value, such as 200. If ISO is set in your camera using its menu, you may have to use the rear joystick/command wheel to change the value. If there is a dedicated ISO button on your camera, you may be able to set it with the front Command Wheel. This is camera-dependent, but important for you to learn. Check your manufacturer's manual if in doubt.
3. Set the Mode wheel to Shutter Priority (Tv or S) and select 1/250 second using the Command Wheel. Push the shutter button halfway, and the camera will take a light reading. Using the display on either the LCD panel or in the viewfinder, you will see the shutter speed you have set

(250) and another number beside it. This is the aperture value or f/stop that the camera has determined is needed for proper exposure. Write down this value.

4. Change the shutter speed to 1/125 second (125 on the display). Keeping the camera aimed at the same scene or object (this is important), note the new aperture value. Refer back to the f/stop chart in Table 1 on page 22. The aperture values you recorded may not match the table exactly, but you should be able to see that the aperture (chosen by the camera) changed by about one f/stop. The aperture value will be higher (larger f/number) because by setting a longer shutter opening (from 1/250 to 1/125 second) the camera will let in twice the amount of light. One f/stop higher in value means the aperture is smaller and letting in half the amount of light to compensate for the slower shutter. In this way, the camera is always ensuring that the exposure is correct. For example, the numbers you see may be 250 5.6 (1/250 second at f/5.6) and 125 8 (1/125 second at f/8) or some other set of aperture values, dependent on the amount of light in the scene.

5. Repeat 3. and 4. using Aperture Priority (Av or A) mode instead, and select f/5.6 with the Command Wheel. Record the shutter speed chosen by the camera. Now select f/8 and record the shutter speed. The shutter speed should have doubled (open twice as long, indicated by a smaller number) at f/8.

6. Leave the camera in Aperture Priority mode and select f/5.6. Note again the shutter speed chosen by the camera. Change the ISO from 200 to 100, and take another reading by pushing the shutter button halfway. Again, the shutter speed should have doubled (open twice as long), because ISO 100 is only half the light sensitivity of ISO 200.

Analysis of Results:

Each of the steps 3. to 6. above are intended to show that doubling or halving shutter speed results in the camera choosing an aperture that is one stop lower (smaller f/number) or one stop higher (larger f/number), respectively, in order to maintain the same exposure.

Changing the aperture instead results in the same relationship (ie. higher f/number requires a slower shutter). Further, doubling or halving the ISO results in halving or doubling the exposure, respectively (ie. double the exposure requires the shutter to be open twice as long or aperture to be changed to a lower f/number to compensate for the camera's sensitivity being halved).

NOTE: The success of this exercise is dependent on the light being relatively constant, the focal length of the zoom lens being fixed at 35mm, and the camera always being aimed at the exact same scene throughout the exercise.

NOTE: If the aperture value is flashing when you are in Shutter Priority mode (some cameras display the phrase 'Low Light' instead) there is not enough light in the scene. Move to a brighter area and restart the exercise.

NOTES:

CHAPTER 5: LENSES AND SENSORS

Of all the accessories you can buy for your camera, lenses are the most important and the most expensive.

In this chapter, characteristics of lenses will be detailed, so you can make informed purchase decisions. Then, sensor sizes will be discussed. If you have already purchased a DSLR, sensor size may be moot since you have no choice in the matter. If, however, you are considering a camera upgrade, you may not want to skip the last topic in this chapter.

Focal Length

In loose terms, focal length is a measure of the distance between the 'optical center' of the lens and the sensor plane. Changing the focal length determines how much the image is magnified on the sensor. Telephoto, normal and wide angle lenses have different focal lengths and therefore different magnification factors.

Focal length is illustrated in a rather simplistic fashion in Figure 5 - 1, which shows a single element lens for demonstration purposes.

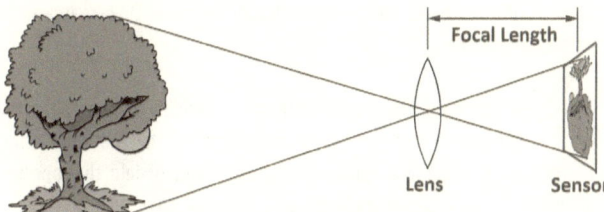

Figure 5 - 1 Focal Length

If we are focused on a tree at infinity (ie. on the horizon), the light rays from the top and bottom of the image will converge within the lens. The distance from the convergence point to the sensor is the focal length. This is specified in millimeters.

In reality, the lenses you buy for your camera have several elements, so the convergence point is not as obvious as in our simple lens. That's not something to be concerned about, because all lenses of the same focal length (that are compatible with your camera) will all behave in the same way. That is, a 50mm focal length lens made by various manufacturers for your camera will all have the same magnification and therefore the same angle of view.

Normal

Our eyes let us perceive an angle of view of about 180° if we look in one direction, but only about 53° or less is in focus. A lens of normal focal length attempts to emulate what we can perceive clearly, so it captures that same 53°angle of view.

As we'll see under the discussion about sensors, normal focal length for a consumer DSLR using an APS-C size sensor is approximately 30 to 33mm.

Wide Angle

Lenses of focal length *shorter* than normal are called wide angle. As the name implies, the angle of view increases. The result is that the magnification factor decreases, so objects appear further away than they would with a normal lens.

A consequence of reducing the focal length below normal is that straight lines start to show curvature. This is why buildings appear to lean when shot with a wide angle lens. The shorter the focal length, the more this distortion becomes apparent. An extreme example is the fisheye lens, which has a very short focal length.

One benefit of shorter focal lengths is that depth of field increases as focal length decreases. Along with the choice of a smaller aperture, this combination results in landscape photos that are in focus from just in front of the camera out to the horizon.

Telephoto

If the focal length of a lens is *longer* than normal, the lens is telephoto. As you might expect, the angle of view decreases and the magnification increases, Objects appear closer than they would with a normal lens.

This type of lens is used frequently by sports and wildlife photographers to get closer to their subject. Another benefit is soft, out-of-focus backgrounds that make the in-focus subject stand out. This is because longer focal lengths *decrease* the depth of field, the opposite to the increased depth of field that wide angle lenses produce.

Zoom Lenses

Lenses that allow us to change the focal length are referred to as zoom lenses. Zooming is usually done by rotating a ring on the lens to align specific focal lengths marked on the ring with a mark on the lens barrel.

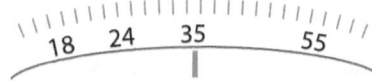

As the ring is rotated, multiple lens elements within the barrel move relative to each other. The separation between these elements change depending upon the selected focal length.

At the longest focal length, these gaps are at their greatest. This results in more light losses within the lens than at the shortest focal length. The maximum aperture achievable at the longest focal length is therefore lower (greater f/number) than at the shortest focal length.

For example, a zoom lens may have a maximum aperture of f/3.5 at the shortest focal length but only f/5.6 at the longest focal length. This range is usually marked somewhere on the zoom lens, often at the front of the lens. In this example, we would see the marking 1:3.5-5.6.

Zoom lenses with maximum aperture that doesn't change with focal length are available, but are usually expensive.

Prime Lenses

A lens with a fixed focal length is called a prime lens. Because of their relatively simple design, their main benefit is more light sensitivity than zoom lenses with complex internal structures. This means that the maximum aperture on a prime lens is greater (lower f/number) than a non-prime lens. Maximum apertures of f/1.2 are fairly common in prime lenses as opposed to f/2.8 or f/3.5 for zoom lenses.

Photographers love their prime lenses for several reasons. Because their maximum apertures are so large, *bokeh* occurs. Distant lights in night scenes look like large colored circles at maximum aperture, which makes a nice background.

Secondly, because larger apertures result in shallow depth of field, portraits taken at maximum aperture have a very soft out-of-focus background which makes their subject stand out.

Large apertures also translate to faster shutter speeds for a given amount of light. This means you can shoot portraits under natural light shortly after the sun sets without the need of a tripod.

Macro Lenses

By strict definition, a macro lens is one that is capable of a magnification of 1:1, or 1x. This means that an object, for example a 1cm diameter marble, will be recorded on the digital sensor at exactly 1cm in diameter, or life size. This has the obvious benefit to photographers of allowing very small objects to be shot at very close range.

While some zoom lenses are advertised as having a macro function, they in fact cannot achieve a 1x magnification. Factors of 0.5 to 0.7x are the best that can typically be achieved.

Prime macro lenses, however, are designed specifically for this function, and can achieve 1x magnification. This allows closeups of insects and flowers. Check the lens specifications before making a purchase, to ensure it can achieve 1x magnification, or 1:1.

The disadvantage of shooting in macro is that depth of field is extremely shallow. Shooting flower detail on a breezy day therefore is a challenge, so moving indoors under artificial light (such as a ring light flash) may be less frustrating.

Sensor Size & Lens Compatibility

There are several different sensor sizes available in DSLR cameras, but by far the most prevalent are APS-C and Full Frame. Even within the APS-C category, there is variation in size that is manufacturer-dependent. For the purposes of discussion here, the Canon APS-C sensor size (22x15mm) will be used, although it should be noted that other brands use a 24x16mm (approximate) sensor for their APS-C cameras.

So who cares what size the sensor is? If you intend to continue using the same camera body and lenses that you've already purchased for years to come, you can probably skip this topic. But if abandoning APS-C in favour of a full frame body is in the cards, the lenses you now have will become useless unless they are designed for full frame.

APS-C versus Full Frame Sensors

Figure 5 - 2 illustrates the difference in size between full frame and Canon APS-C sensors. Note that the full frame sensor is exactly the same size as a 35mm film negative.

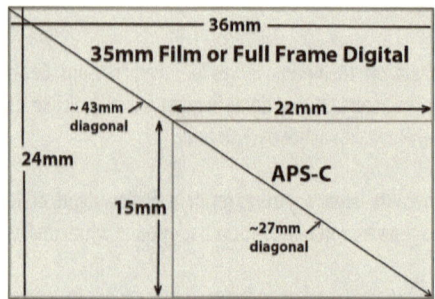

Figure 5 - 2 Sensor Size Comparison

While APS-C and full frame sensors can have the same resolution (eg. 21 megapixels), the full frame sensor is superior because it has larger pixels. In other words, each sensor is comprised of 21 million pixels (picture elements), but the larger pixel size means they can gather more light by virtue of more surface area. This leads to lower 'noise' at any given ISO setting because the camera's electronics do not have to amplify the sensor signals (and contribute their own inherent noise) to the same degree that they do in an APS-C camera. This is a fundamental reason for the full frame body's higher price tag.

Image Circle and Lens Types

Think of the camera lens as a projector. It collects the light from the scene being photographed and projects it onto the back of the camera body, and onto the sensor. Because the lens elements are round, the scene is projected as an 'image circle'.

The sensor, however, is rectangular, so the image circle diameter must be at least as big as the diagonal measurement of the sensor. If not, the image will not cover the sensor completely and the corners will be dark. This is called vignetting.

Manufacturers provide two different types of lenses for DSLRs: one for full frame and one for the smaller sensors such as APS-C. The image circles for each are illustrated in Figure 5 - 3.

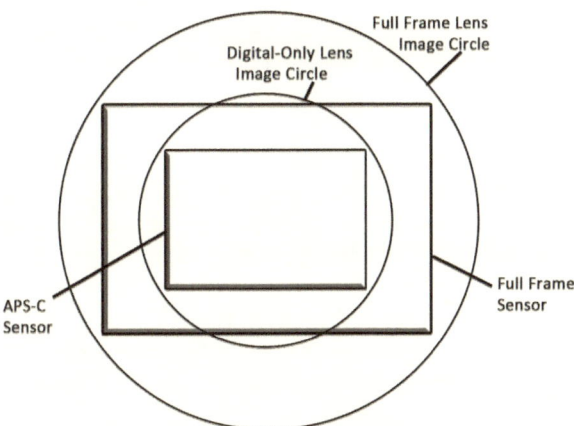

Figure 5 - 3 Image Circle Comparison

Note that lenses designed for smaller sensors are often referred to a 'digital only'. This is a bit of an unfortunate misnomer that likely came about in the transition from 35mm film to APS-C digital lenses, in order to distinguish between the image circle provided by each. In fact, lenses designed for 35mm film cameras work just fine on full frame *digital* cameras from the same manufacturer.

Using Canon and Nikon lenses for example, for APS-C cameras the lenses are designated EF-S (Canon) or DX (Nikon). Full frame lenses are designated EF (Canon) or FX (Nikon). Lens manufacturers have intentionally made the mounts for APS-C lenses incompatible with full frame bodies to prevent you from using lenses that will create vignetted pictures. The other reason is that APS-C lenses physically extend further into the camera body and interfere with the mirror on full frame bodies when it flips up during picture taking.

Using full frame lenses on APS-C bodies, however, is completely acceptable. Because full frame lenses have a bigger image circle, they more than adequately cover the APS-C size sensor. For this reason, if you are considering a lens purchase, you may want to spring for the (albeit more expensive) full frame version so that you can use it on both types of bodies.

Crop Factor

Now, imagine using the same *full frame* prime lens on both an APS-C body and a full frame body. The lens is compatible with both, but the results will be noticeably different.

Figure 5 - 4 (top) shows an image containing dots and an X projected by a full frame lens onto a full frame sensor. The X is completely captured by the sensor and part of each of the middle four dots are captured at the edges.

Placing that same lens on an APS-C camera results in only the X being captured, and in fact, filling more of the frame than in the full frame camera. The focal length has not changed, so that does not account for the difference. Rather, the APS-C sensor occupies a smaller portion of the image circle than the full frame sensor, so it only 'sees' a smaller part of the image projected by the lens.

Note that this effect is the same as zooming in on the image captured by the full frame sensor until the X fills the frame. This difference in *apparent* focal length between using the same lens on an APS-C camera versus a full frame camera is called the Crop Factor. Using the Canon sensor sizes for APS-C and full frame sensors, this factor is approximately 1.6 times.

To state this simply, you can use the same full frame prime lens on both sensor sizes, but expect the image to frame quite differently. Stated another way, using a 50mm prime lens on a full frame camera will frame the image exactly the same way as using a 31mm lens (50 divided by 1.6) on an APS-C camera.

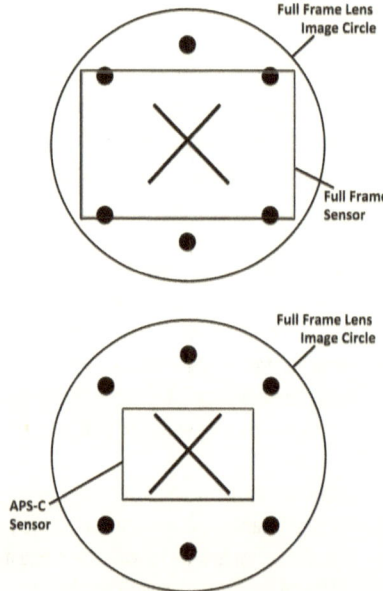

Figure 5 - 4 Crop Factor

In case your head hasn't blown up yet, I'll state it yet another way. For the same sensor size (let's assume APS-C), using a 50mm full frame prime lens (eg. Canon EF) and a 50mm APS-C prime lens (eg. Canon EF-S) on the same camera will result in the same image size. As long as the focal length is the same, all lenses of that focal length will provide the same image *on the same camera body*. Conversely, if one prime lens is used alternately on APS-C and full frame cameras, the image will change in size by 1.6x.

CHAPTER 6: WHITE BALANCE AND COLOR SPACE

What is White Balance?

Imagine taking photographs at a wedding and all the shots of the bride's dress have either an orange or bluish cast instead of appearing white. This means that the white balance in the camera has not interpreted the light correctly.

As the name implies, Auto White Balance reads the light coming through the lens and automatically attempts to balance the red, green and blue sensor channels so that white looks white and that pure shades of grey do not have a color cast. It does this by compensating for the color temperature of the light.

Color temperature, measured in degrees Kelvin (°K), varies with light source. Daylight tends to be bluish or colder, so its color temperature (counter-intuitively, perhaps) is higher than incandescent light bulbs, which tend to be reddish or warm. Typically, overcast daylight is about 6500°K while incandescent bulbs are usually 3000°K on average.

White, or any true shade of grey, will have equal amounts of red, green and blue. This can be verified by opening a photo in editing software, placing the cursor over a known white/near-white then a grey part of the image and reading the red, green and blue values. For example, you may see something like (250,250,250) or (128,128,128), respectively. If the three numbers differ greatly from each other, the white balance is not correct.

White Balance Presets

In situations where you will be shooting under a particular type of light, you can choose a preset white balance rather than Auto. These presets have names like Daylight, Cloudy, Shade, Fluorescent and Incandescent.

The benefit to using presets is that the white balance will not vary even if you have a slight contribution from a different light source (eg. window light spilling into a room predominantly lit by incandescent bulbs). Using the Incandescent preset in this case may provide a better white balance than Auto, which may get fooled by the window light.

Just remember to change the white balance setting when you move from one light source to another!

Custom White Balance

If you are working under consistent lighting conditions, such as in a studio, you can create a white balance preset that is customized to that lighting.

While the procedure may change with camera model, here is an example of how you would set a custom white balance:

1.   Under your specific lighting conditions, take a photo of a neutral grey or white surface. You can use Auto White Balance if you wish because the Custom setting will correct it later for any white balance errors. Make sure the surface is evenly lit by the light, and fill the frame completely with it.

2.   Go into the camera's menu and find Custom White Balance. Check your manual if uncertain. You will be prompted to select a photo to use for the Custom setting. Choose the photo you just took and press the Set button to store your selection.

3.   Find your White Balance presets. These will either be in the menu or on a dedicated WB button. One of the presets will be called Custom. Select it, and you can now shoot under your lighting setup. This will result in consistent and accurate white balance as long as the light doesn't change. Remember to reset the White Balance to Auto or another preset when finished.

Correcting White Balance in Software

White imbalances when using Auto White Balance most frequently occur when the subject is in mixed light. The room lit by incandescent bulbs but with some window light is the example used previously. The camera has to choose settings that it calculates to be correct in order to make white look white. Chances are that one of the light sources will dominate and white objects will end up with a color cast created by the other light source. This can be fixed in software.

Most photo editing software provides a means of reading the red, green and blue channel levels when the cursor is placed anywhere in the image. Further, some have a simple slider control to allow you to correct white balance.

If you know that a particular area in the image should be pure white, black or a neutral grey, place the cursor over it and read the R,G and B values. If they vary greatly (eg. 250, 236, 220), then adjust the white balance until they are within a few points of each other (eg. 252, 254, 253 is acceptable for a near-white object).

The Color Space Setting – sRGB vs. Adobe RGB

Color Space (sometimes called color gamut) refers to the range of colors that the camera is required to record. By default, the factory typically sets this parameter to sRGB (smaller triangle in Figure 6 - 1).

Most consumer four color inkjet printers have a rather limited color gamut that they can reproduce. If the camera is set to sRGB, the implication is that the image you record will contain a similar color range to the home printer's capability.

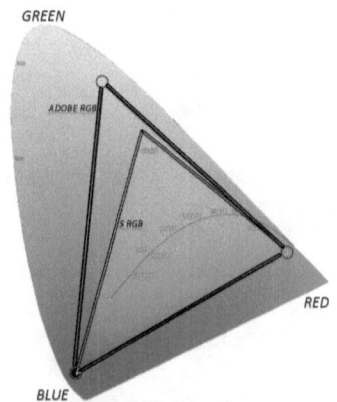

Figure 6 - 1 Color Spaces

If you intend to go 'pro', however, you would be better served changing the Color Space setting in your camera's menu to Adobe RGB (larger triangle in Figure 6 - 1). This gamut is wider than that of sRGB, meaning it will record a wider range of color hues. Because publishers have the capability of printing a wider gamut than the home printer, they will generally insist that you submit images created with Adobe RGB.

There is an ongoing controversy on the Internet over which Color Space to use. The consensus seems to be that if you are printing at home or intend to publish on the Internet, use sRGB. You can, however, always convert in software from Adobe RGB to sRGB if your printing results are unsatisfactory. The reverse unfortunately is not advisable when submitting to a publisher.

Photographic Exercise 5

Let's see how intentionally (or accidentally) using the wrong white balance can affect our results.

1. Using the camera's menu, find White Balance. Some cameras have a dedicated button for this (WB). Check your camera's manual if in doubt.
2. Set up the camera to shoot a specific scene (preferably on a tripod so the lighting in the frame is consistent) and leave it there.
3. Take a shot using Auto White Balance (AWB). Try some of the other White Balance presets (ie. fluorescent, incandescent, cloudy bright) and take a shot for each.
4. Review the shots. You should see a difference in the color, particularly on skin tones.
5. Choose Auto White Balance again. Now, take a shot of something *without* color cast, such as a grey card or white piece of paper, and completely fill the frame with it. In the camera's menu, go to Custom White Balance. You will be prompted to choose a photo. Scroll to the one you just took and accept it. Now choose Custom white balance from your camera's presets. Any pictures you take with that preset will now achieve an accurate white balance if shot under the same lighting conditions that you shot the grey or white card. This setting is not commonly used, but may be helpful if you are shooting under mixed lighting (ie. indoor + outdoor) where Auto White Balance may get confused. Don't forget to return the preset to Auto White Balance when finished.
6. In the camera's menu, find Color Space or Color Gamut. Note that by default, sRGB will probably be chosen. Select Adobe RGB instead, so that your camera is recording a wider range of colors.

Analysis:

In most cases, leave the camera in Auto White Balance setting, because the camera's computer is generally good at determining the right setting. The goal with white balance, as the name implies, is to ensure that white (or for that matter, any shade of grey) is recorded as neutral. This means there will be equal amounts of red, green and blue. This can be verified in photo editing software by placing the cursor over, say, a white wedding dress and confirming that the displayed values of red, green and blue (on a scale of 0-255) are approximately equal.

In mixed light situations (daylight coming through a window and incandescent lights overhead), perfect white balance may never be achieved over the entire image, but a Custom white balance may help you get closer than if you relied on Auto White Balance. Regardless of your WB setting, chances are you may have to spend some time doing white balance correction in software, especially for tricky lighting scenarios.

NOTES:

CHAPTER 7: RESOLUTION AND FILE TYPES

Your DSLR allows you to choose the resolution, quality and file type you wish to use when you record your images onto the memory card. Your choices will determine how much memory each image will require, and therefore the maximum number of shots you can store on one card.

Compressed Files – JPEG

Chances are, your camera was set up at the factory to record in JPEG format, by default. For most consumers who simply want to email their images or print them at home, this format is perfectly suitable.

So, what is a JPEG file, anyway? In order to save memory when recording images, the JPEG format was devised to compress the data it records. It does this by throwing away some of the image data. Because human visual perception is less sensitive to color changes than brightness changes, in a nutshell the JPEG compression algorithm throws away much of the color transition information in the image. It is called a lossy compression method, which has consequences depending on what we do with the file later on.

Let's assume you were to open a JPEG file in photo editing software, make changes to it, save it, close it, then open it again. If you were to repeat this process several times, eventually you would notice degradation in image quality. This is because every time you save and close the file, you have thrown away more data, even when saving at the highest quality level that the software allows.

If heavy, repeated editing is not going to be performed on an image, however, the image that comes straight from the camera can be of very high quality in JPEG format.

Choosing Image Size (Resolution)

Think of your camera's recorded image as being made up of dots called pixels (picture elements). The more dots, the higher the resolution, or the ability for the camera to record fine details. This is typically expressed as the number of pixels along the longest dimension of the image by the number of pixels along the shortest dimension of the image. For instance, a 17.9 megapixel sensor is capable of creating images that are 5184 by 3456 pixels. (5184x3456 is 17,915,904)

If you wanted to save space on your memory card, you could choose to record at a resolution lower than 5184 by 3456 pixels given in this example. To determine how to do this, you may have to crack open your specific camera's manual, or just go hunting through your camera's menu for Quality or Image Size. There, you may encounter various 'L', 'M' or 'S' icons. Often, the pixel dimensions are also displayed, so that you can tell which setting gives the highest resolution. L is the highest resolution, M is medium and S is the smallest.

Choosing a Compression Level (Quality)

For shooting in JPEG, once you have chosen a resolution, you can set the amount of compression. If you need to be able to fit the maximum number of images on a memory card, look for Quality or Image Quality in the menu system and choose the lowest quality. Lower quality settings use the most amount of compression, and are either designated by an icon with a stairstep edge, by a word like Normal or Basic, or by one or two stars (camera-dependent).

The highest quality setting may be an icon with a smooth edge, by a word like Fine, or by three stars. These JPEG images will take up the most space on a memory card, but the highest quality setting is recommended if you anticipate doing some minor editing in software, or printing enlargements.

RAW or NEF

While navigating through the Image Quality and Image Size menus, you may have noticed a setting called either RAW or NEF.

As opposed to JPEG, these formats use no compression whatsoever. The most popular photo editing software packages will open them and provide controls for correcting white balance and a host of other image parameters in a dedicated interface. Software packaged with the camera may also allow you to change the 'Picture Style' you shot the original RAW or NEF image in, without any degradation.

These file formats by default are recorded at the highest resolution that the camera is capable of. There is a price to pay, of course. RAW and NEF files are bigger than JPEGs, so you can't store as many on a memory card. With today's cavernous cards, however, this is rarely a concern.

Once you bring a RAW or NEF file into your photo editing software, you can save it to another uncompressed format, like TIFF. That way, you can edit the image over several sessions without fear of degradation from saving and opening the file multiple times. Uncompressed formats are a must for photographers who want to spend time perfecting their images in software. Keep in mind that you can always save a separate JPEG copy if you want to provide smaller file to someone.

But what if you're shooting on location and a client or friend wants instant copies that they can view easily on their computer? You can choose RAW+JPEG or NEF+JPEG instead, which will record two file types simultaneously. Your friend gets the (unedited) JPEGs but you have the RAW or NEF versions for editing later. Because you are recording two files at a time, this will definitely reduce the number of images you can fit on a memory card.

Photographic Exercise 6

If you haven't already learned how, let's set the recording file type, resolution and quality. Every camera manufacturer approaches this differently. Refer to your camera's manual under 'image quality' or 'recording quality'.

1.   Look in your camera's menu for Quality or Image Size/Quality (or your camera's equivalent).
2.   Choose the highest resolution JPEG setting (usually an L preceded by a curved icon or just an L). Note that the resolution (pixel dimensions of the form aaaa X bbbb) is sometimes displayed as well (camera-dependent).
3.   At this highest resolution, notice that you have more than one compression level to choose from. Select the lowest compression/highest quality version. The choices may be Fine, Normal and Basic (Nikon), in which case, you would choose Fine. For Canon, choose the icon (in front of the L) that has the smoothest curve. For Pentax, choose 3 stars. You have now set your camera to shoot in JPEG mode at the highest resolution and quality level.
4.   Try setting the choices for RAW or NEF and RAW+JPEG or NEF+JPEG.(Your camera may not display the choices exactly the same way, but the meaning is the same). If you wanted to shoot in RAW or NEF only, select one of those. If you select RAW+JPEG or NEF+JPEG, the camera will store one of each (with the JPEG automatically set to highest resolution and lowest compression/highest quality).

NOTES:

CHAPTER 8: LIGHT AND COMPOSITION

While the intent of this book is primarily to help the reader gain confidence in using their DSLR, some concepts presented here will help in producing better images through a fundamental understanding of light and composition.

Ambient Light and the Effect of Time of Day

So often, we are compelled to take photographs in mid-day. That's because weddings and family gatherings take place then, and the kids are most active in the daytime.

If you recall the discussion about color temperature in Chapter 6 (What is White Balance? on page 39), it was stated that there is a strong blue cast in daytime light. Subjectively, this results in less balanced color content dominated by a cold blue hue. Coupling that with a high overhead sun which casts long shadows under eye sockets, noses and chins, taking shots of people at this time of day results in unflattering portraits.

If you have to shoot in the middle of the day, overcast skies are an improvement. Because the clouds diffuse the sun's light, shadows become soft or non-existent. This is a preferred scenario for outdoor portraiture, although the color temperature is still very high.

Travel and landscape photographers instead prefer to shoot during 'magic hour' or 'magic time'. This refers to the hour around sunrise and again around sunset. Because the sun is much

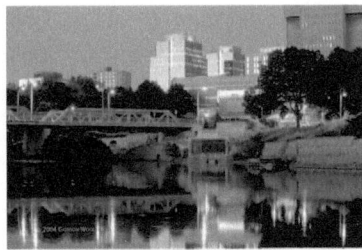

Figure 8 - 1 Evening Magic Hour

lower in the sky, it is filtered through more of the earth's atmosphere than it would be if directly overhead. Its light takes on a warmer hue (lower color temperature) and creates long, dramatic horizontal shadows. Colors tend to be more saturated, because scenery is no longer bathed in extremely strong blue mid-day light. Skies take on an inky look, particularly when facing away from a sunset (Figure 8 - 1).

While a sun that is low in the sky at magic hour may cause squinting at times, it is still the preferred time for fashion and automobile photography because of the dramatic, warm light it provides.

> **STARTING TIP:** If shooting landscapes at magic hour, always use aperture priority mode and set the aperture as small as possible to maximize depth of field. f/16 to f/22 will achieve this. Use a tripod or image stabilization because shutter speeds slower than 1/30th of a second (which may cause motion blur) will possibly be required in low light. If doing a fashion or portrait shoot instead, use wide apertures (f/8 or wider) to ensure faster shutter speeds and softer backgrounds.

A note about the difference between morning and evening magic hours. While most people would prefer not to get out of a warm bed to experience the sunrise, it has one benefit over sunset. Over relatively warm bodies of water such as lakes and rivers, the moisture evaporating from them is cooled by the descending night air until the moisture condenses into a fog or mist. This effect is most prevalent on autumn mornings, and can add drama to an image (Figure 8 - 2).

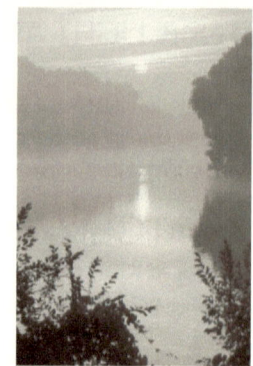

Figure 8 - 2 Morning Magic Hour

Artificial Light as Fill

For those times when we have no choice but to shoot at mid-day, using a flash as a 'fill' light is a good remedy. Turning on the flash outdoors helps to fade the shadows cast by the sun on the face. It also helps overcome underexposure of the subject if there is a strong backlight.

Accessory Flash vs. Pop-Up Flash

Your DSLR has a built in flash that pops up in any of the Creative Modes when you press the flash button. It is totally up to you whether or not you want to use flash in a particular scenario.

You can also purchase an accessory flash that is compatible with your camera model. It fastens to the hot shoe on the top of the camera, and prevents the built in flash from popping up once it is attached. Some benefits of using an accessory flash over the built in flash are:

- Greater physical separation between the camera and the flash head, which helps eliminate interference or shadows cast by large diameter or long lenses.
- Greater maximum power output capability and a greater range of power output adjustment.
- The ability to separate the flash from the camera and trigger it remotely, thereby controlling the nature of the shadow cast by the flash behind the subject.
- The ability to easily attach light modifiers, such as color filters and diffusers.
- The ability to swivel the head to 'bounce' light off walls or ceilings to diffuse or soften the light.
- The ability to use high speed sync (see Flash Sync Speeds on page 29), if that function is provided by the accessory flash.

Choosing a Creative Mode for Outdoor Fill Flash

Let's compare the three semi-automatic Creative Modes (Program, Aperture Priority and Shutter Priority) when using fill flash. The results can differ, even under the same lighting conditions.

When using Aperture Priority or Shutter Priority, the camera reads the ambient light in the scene as if there were no flash. This means it will determine exposure using evaluative or matrix metering and expose the scene to an average 18% grey (see The Meaning of 18% Grey on page 16). Then the flash fires and *adds* light to the scene. This can result in slight overexposure of the subject since it was already properly exposed before the flash fired.

To verify this for yourself, try taking a shot in either Aperture or Shutter Priority modes in a dark room using the flash. You'll notice when you press the shutter button, the shutter stays open for a long time before firing the flash. That's because the camera is trying to expose the dark room first, based on the low ambient light it reads.

If we use Program mode instead, the camera uses the light reflected from the flash as its main source for determining exposure. The benefit this has in outdoor fill flash situations is that the flash light plus the ambient light bouncing off your subject is used to determine exposure, rather than primarily the background ambient light. This results in a more accurate exposure of your subject.

Again, you can verify this in a dark room, this time using Program mode and flash. When you press the shutter button, the flash fires immediately, and the recorded image uses only the light from the flash to expose the room.

Using Flash Exposure Compensation to Balance Light

As explained in Flash Exposure Compensation on page 4, the light output of the flash (whether built in or accessory) can be controlled independently of the exposure setting on the camera. This gives you the opportunity to balance the light from the flash falling on your subject with the outdoor background ambient light.

Typically, you can either adjust flash exposure compensation using the controls on the accessory flash, or through the menu system in the camera. For the built in flash, this can only be adjusted through the camera's menu. The numbers on the scale correspond to stops, so adjust-

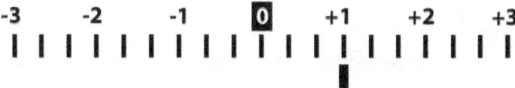

ing compensation by +1 results in a one stop increase in flash output, or a doubling of light intensity.

The Softbox

Direct light from a flash is very harsh, and can result in hard shadows. Using adhesive Velcro™ strips around the flash head, a foldable softbox can be added and removed easily.

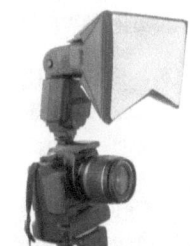

Like the clouds on an overcast day, the softbox diffuses the light source, resulting in less distinct shadows. This is similar to the effect provided by softboxes and umbrellas used

Figure 8 - 3 Softbox on an Accessory Flash

with studio strobes, but with a less pronounced effect because of the smaller physical size.

You can get a similar effect with the built in flash by using a tissue or gauze over the flash head. Because of the smaller surface area of the built in flash head, however, it is not as effective as using a softbox on an accessory flash.

Reflectors as Fill

If you have an assistant or you've grown a third arm, a foldable reflector makes a nice alternative to fill flash. These are typically available in a format that allows you to choose gold, silver or white. You simply use the sun to reflect light onto your subject to fill in daytime shadows or to make your subject pop against the background. Skin tones are usually complemented quite well by a gold reflector (Figure 8 - 4), although white also works well.

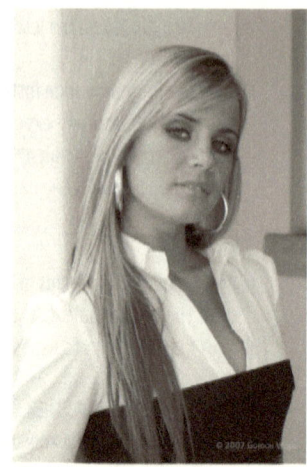

Figure 8 - 4 Gold Reflector on Skin Tones

If you have a light stand, you can buy a special arm that clamps to it and has spring clips to hold the edges of the reflector. That way, you can work solo.

Diffusers

Some foldable reflector discs include a white diffuser sheet. This can be held above your subject to soften the harsh light of direct sun. It has a similar effect to being under a white marquee tent.

Composition Tips

There is a natural tendency when taking photographs to center our subject and fire away. After all, our job is just to capture something, right?

Think about a photograph that moved you. It probably had outstanding lighting, but it was probably also composed in a compelling way. Here's a handful of composition methods that great photographers use instinctively.

The Rule of Thirds

Have a look at a landscape photograph shot by a professional. Where is the horizon - in the middle of the photograph? Absolutely not.

The Rule of Thirds states that you should place the horizon either one third of the way up from the bottom or one third of the way down from the top. Your choice depends on whether you want to feature a dramatic sky or an interesting foreground. Placing it in the middle is boring because your eye doesn't know where the point of interest in the photograph is situated.

Diagonals

You need to capture the attention of the viewer with your photograph. If you're shooting a landscape, travel or architectural scene, lines that are parallel to the edge of the photograph do nothing to draw your eye in.

Try to introduce a diagonal line somewhere in the scene. For instance, instead of shooting a fence or wall face-on, shoot it at a slight angle. The converging lines created by introducing perspective will generate a diagonal for you.

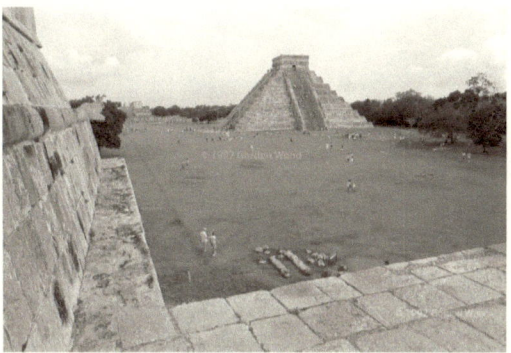

Figure 8 - 5 Rule of Thirds + Diagonals

Figure 8 - 5 shows how both the Rule of Thirds and diagonals (created by the foreground walls) can be combined in one photograph.

Offsetting the Subject

As mentioned, when shooting a subject we are compelled to place them in the center of the frame. For portraits, there is nothing wrong with that. But if we want to convey a sense of place or imply action, try to offset your subject to one side of center.

You can balance the scene with something on the opposite side of the frame (ie. a destination that the subject is moving toward or a dramatic open sky). An example would be a child blowing soap bubbles from a dispenser. By placing them against one side of the frame, the stream of bubbles extending to the other side of the frame and up into the sky gives a sense of space and action.

NOTES:

CHAPTER 9: FILTERS

Some purists believe that using filters on a camera is blasphemy. Their contention is that if you can't make an image compelling using the available light, you're cheating.

I'm of a different mind. Photography is an art form. For over a century, photographers have used the darkroom to tweak the density, contrast and tonal balance in their prints. Today, we can even emulate the effect of filters in software, so if we should have used a filter on the camera but neglected to do so, we have an opportunity to correct it in post production.

There is a huge variety of filters available. In this chapter, I'll touch on the ones that I think are the most important. Ignore the nay-sayers - jump right in and try some!

Systems versus Thread-On Glass Filters

If you look at the front of your lenses, you will notice that there is a thread. This is how you attach filters or filter systems to the lens. Hopefully, most of your lenses will have the same diameter thread, because that means you can use the same filters on all your lenses. The thread diameter is

Ø58mm

in millimeters, and is marked somewhere on the lens in the format shown at left. When purchasing filters or filter holders, you will need to buy them with the same thread diameter as marked on the lens.

Systems use adapter rings that thread onto the lens (Figure 9 - 1). A filter holder slides onto the ring and allows you to insert a wide variety of pre-cut filter materials or try something you make up yourself (such as a mask shape). The benefit, as we'll see with graduated filters, is that you can position the filter material by sliding it up/down/left/right to get the desired effect.

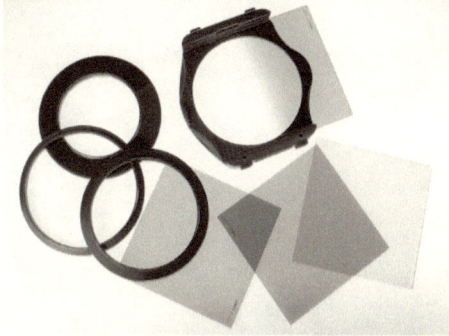

Figure 9 - 1 Filter System Components

The disadvantage with systems is that the filter materials available for them is often made of plastic or resin. My experience has been that these materials can create a slight softening effect because plastic is optically inferior to glass found in thread-on filters. Plastic is also more subject to scratching or hazing which will eventually affect image quality.

UV

When film cameras ruled the photography world, ultraviolet (UV) filters were considered essential. Because films were more sensitive to UV light than current digital sensors, a UV filter was used to eliminate the haziness introduced by UV wavelengths in daylight.

Today, photographers often install a UV filter on their lenses to protect the lens surface rather than to filter out UV light. Keep in mind that adding filters of any kind to the front of the lens adds two surfaces that can introduce internal reflections. This can result in light 'flares' or bright spots, particularly when shooting in the direction of the sun.

Use of a UV filter is therefore up to the photographer's discretion, but is certainly not essential.

Polarizing

Perhaps the most useful filter in my camera bag is the polarizing filter. Think of how polarized sunglasses work. When you wear them, contrast improves and glare off of surfaces like water is virtually eliminated.

Light is an electromagnetic wave. As a result, its electric and magnetic fields are oriented in a specific way. When light from the sun is filtered by the earth's atmosphere, this orientation becomes random throughout the sky.

If we were to filter the randomly polarized light at the camera so that only waves of a specific orientation were allowed through, the light from the blue sky would appear darker because we have removed some of the randomly-polarized light coming from it. If we have an object in the same scene that essentially has a solid surface, the light from the sun that reflects off it would be polarized uniformly and pass through the filter more easily. The result is an image with more contrast: the sky is darkened but the smooth parts of the object are virtually unchanged.

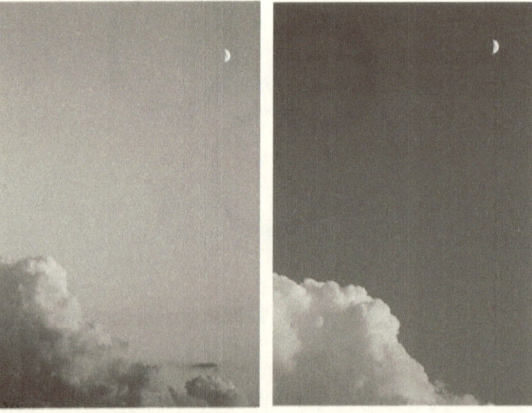

Figure 9 - 2 Polarizing Filter Effect

In Figure 9 - 2, the image on the left was taken without a polarizing filter. Compare that with the polarized image on the right. Notice that the smooth surfaces of the cloud are unchanged but the sky has noticeably darkened. In other words, the contrast has increased. Travel and landscape photographers use a polarizing filter specifically to make white puffy clouds stand out against the sky to add a dramatic element.

The polarizing filter has two rings. One threads onto the front of the lens, while the other rotates on the mounting ring. By rotating this ring, the amount of polarization can be varied.

Note that the polarization effect is greatest when the camera is aimed at 90° to the sun. The effect gradually diminishes to zero as the camera is aimed toward the sun or with the sun directly behind the camera.

Neutral Density

If we want to introduce motion blur into our photographs (see Slow Shutter Speeds on page 28), the strong light intensity in mid-day may not allow a sufficiently slow shutter speed. By adding a neutral density filter, we can reduce the amount of light coming into the camera and force a slower shutter speed.

This filter is like a smoked piece of glass that is available in different densities. An example is the solid grey filter at the bottom of Figure 9 - 1. The term 'neutral' implies that there is no color cast to the filter - it simply attenuates light. Several filters can be stacked by threading one on top of the other to achieve even greater light reduction. Densities are specified in stops. That is, adding a one stop filter to the camera will force either halving of the shutter speed or opening of the aperture by one full f/stop in order to maintain exposure.

Normally, choosing a very small aperture (eg. f/22) will force a slower shutter speed (for a fixed ISO value). In daylight, this may not be enough to force the shutter to stay open for a second or more. In Figure 4 - 2, a neutral density filter was used for that very reason. A long exposure is needed to make the moving water look blurry and smooth. For landscape photographers, this is an ideal scenario because the small aperture yields a greater depth of field while the neutral density filter helps ensure motion blur at the same time.

Graduated

Landscape photographs are typically comprised of sky and foreground (remember the Rule of Thirds?). In simple terms, the foreground reflects light from the sky. If the foreground is shaded by a row of trees, for example, there will be a great difference between the light in the sky and that reflected from the foreground.

In this scenario, the camera's sensor may have difficulty recording everything from shadow detail in the foreground to highlight detail in the clouds because of its limited dynamic range (see Chapter 2: Exposure on page 9). What is needed is a filter that will darken the sky while leaving the foreground alone. That way, all information in the scene can fit within the dynamic range of the sensor. That's what a graduated filter does.

Think of a piece of glass that is tinted at its top end, and it gradually (or abruptly depending on type) lightens up until there is no tint at its center or below. By placing it in a holder (as in Figure 9 - 1), the position of the transition point between light and dark can be placed at the horizon in our photograph by sliding it up and down in the holder. The sky is now darkened by the tint while the foreground remains unfiltered.

Graduated filters are available with neutral tint, or you can buy them with a color tint to add drama to the sky. For example, a magenta-tinted graduated filter was used in Figure 9 - 3 to darken and color the sky.

One caution when using graduated filters is that they are not suitable for all scenarios. For instance, you would not use one if photographing skyscrapers, because placing the transition point through the middle of the building would look obvious, if not ridiculous.

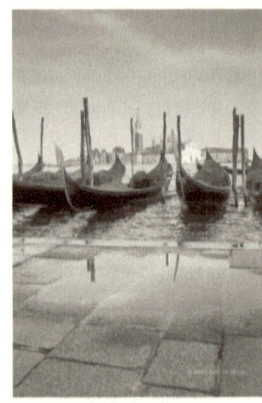

Figure 9 - 3 Graduated Filter Example

Warming

In What is White Balance? on page 39, the concept of color temperature and the cold blue light of mid-day was introduced. This light produces unsatisfactory results because everything in the scene is bathed in blue light. Vegetation, for example, loses some of its natural hue.

A warming filter blocks much of the blue light and lets light of a lower color temperature (orange-red) through. If forced into shooting in the middle of the day, using this filter will produce more pleasing results.

Cooling

Remember the discussion on Magic Hour? The light at this time is warmer than at mid-day, which results in more color intensity and contrast.

But what if this reddish evening light was too much for your taste? By adding a cooling filter, you can reduce the red intensity while restoring some of the cold blue mid-day hue.

An alternative use for this filter is employed by cinematographers. By intentionally underexposing through a blue cooling filter, a moonlit night scene can be emulated.

CHAPTER 10: NIGHT PHOTOGRAPHY

This form of photography implies long time exposures of several seconds to several minutes (or even hours!). The subjects can range from cityscapes illuminated by street and building lights to meteors streaking over the night sky.

Equipment You'll Need

- First and foremost, use a a stable tripod. Without one, any exposures longer than about 1/30th of a second will be blurry.

    An important tip: If you are using a lens with image stabilization, switch it OFF. While some of the newer lenses with this feature can detect whether or not the camera is stationary, older image stabilization systems will actually 'twitch' when on a tripod and introduce blur.

- Shutter release. This is a wired device that plugs into the camera and functions the same as the shutter button on the camera. The difference is that you can activate the shutter without jarring the camera during exposure. An added feature is the ability to lock the shutter without having to physically hold it down. This is very helpful when making exposures of several minutes' length.

- A timer. For exposures longer than 30 seconds, you will be using Manual mode and setting the shutter speed to BULB. This setting means that the shutter will stay open as long as the shutter button or shutter release is held down. Chances are, the camera will give you a timer indication on the LCD panel of how long you've left the shutter open. If your camera doesn't do this, you may have to time the exposure by other means.

Before you go, make sure you have a fully charged battery and maybe a spare. Long exposures require the mirror to stay up for long periods, and also require the camera to do more processing of the image than at normal shutter speeds.

Long Exposure Noise Reduction

For long time exposures, electronic noise generated by the sensor system in the camera is recorded along with your image. This manifests itself as random bright spots that fill the picture.

Fortunately, camera manufacturers provide a setting that subtracts these spots during the processing of the final image. This is an essential function, particularly if your exposures exceed about 1 second. You may have to consult your manual to find out how to set it, but it is likely a Custom Function setting. Leaving it set to ON indefinitely will not affect your shots taken at shutter speeds shorter than 1 second.

The downside to using this function is that the processing time after the shot is taken is usually as long as the time the shutter was open. This means long wait times between shots, particularly for exposures that run into minutes in length, but means the difference between a useful shot and a useless one.

Choosing the Right Creative Mode

There are three scenarios that will be outlined here:
- Time exposures using available continuous light (eg. street or building lighting)
- Time exposures combined with flash
- Night sky photography

Night Photography Using Available Light

In urban areas, available subjects are plentiful at night. Unfortunately, the available light can be from various sources: sodium street lamps, neon signs, fluorescent building lights and incandescent floodlights. White balance may become an issue.

If one type of light source is dominant, use a white balance preset for that light (eg. Fluorescent). If it's a mixture, you may want to stay with Auto White Balance and make any corrections in software later.

For this type of photography, you can use any of the Creative Modes. If achieving depth of field is a concern, though, choose Aperture Priority and select a small aperture (high f/number). The camera will then read the light and automatically determine a shutter speed.

If the light is too low and the shutter speed flashes on the LCD panel and in the viewfinder, a shutter speed longer than 30 seconds (at the aperture you have set) is required. You may have to settle for less depth of field with a wider aperture (smaller f/number). If that's not acceptable, you will need to use Manual mode instead, and use the Command Wheel to set the shutter speed to BULB. This is usually just past the 30" setting. Don't forget to set your aperture in Manual mode as well.

Since the camera doesn't know how long you are going to leave the shutter open in BULB, the bar graph on the LCD panel (see Manual (M) on page 15) will not help you determine exposure. Instead, start with an aperture of f/8 and take a couple of exposures longer than 30 seconds by holding down the shutter release as long as needed and compare the results.

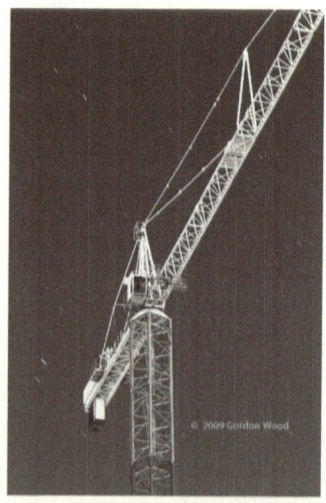

Figure 10 - 1 Night Exposure Using Available Light

Review the histograms when you play back the shots to determine which exposure length gave the best average exposure. If you need more depth of field, use a higher f/number and lengthen the exposure time.

Figure 10 - 1 is an example of a time exposure using sodium street lamps as a light source. The exposure was approximately one minute, resulting in short star trails around the crane as a result of the earth's rotation.

Night Photography Using Flash

This type of photography is an extension of available light shooting, except we now want to include a subject in the foreground and use flash to illuminate them.

Recall that Aperture or Shutter Priority are the modes of choice if you want the background to be exposed properly when using a flash on your subject (see Choosing a Creative Mode for Outdoor Fill Flash on page 48). Also, by choosing a wide aperture (smaller f/number) in Aperture Priority, you can intentionally reduce the depth of field so that lights in the background form *bokeh* patterns.

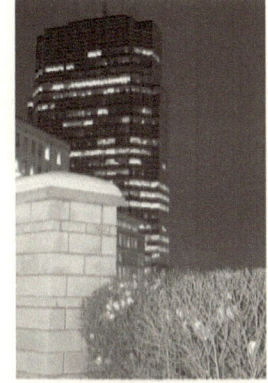

Figure 10 - 2 Night Exposure with Flash using Aperture or Shutter Priority

If it is more important to have greater depth of field, choose a smaller aperture in Aperture Priority. Keep in mind that this will force a slower shutter speed. The downside to longer exposures is that your subject may not hold perfectly still while the shutter stays open. When the flash fires and illuminates your subject, you may see the flash-lit subject with a 'ghost' behind them on the final image, if they moved during the long exposure. This would not be a problem if taking architectural images at night, unless trees are blowing in the breeze. An example is shown in Figure 10 - 2.

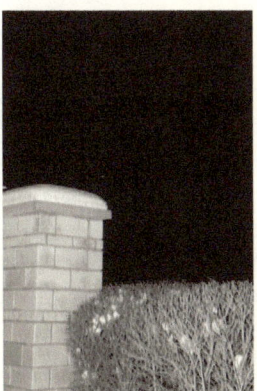

Figure 10 - 3 Night Exposure with Flash using Program

Using Program mode at night with flash will produce a different result. Recall that this mode mainly uses the flash reflected from the foreground subject as the means by which it meters the light. As a result, it does not attempt to expose the background properly, resulting in the subject being properly exposed against a relatively dark background (Figure 10 - 3 - taken right after Figure 10 - 2). For this reason, Aperture and Shutter Priority are the preferred semi-automatic modes for night photography.

Night Sky Photography

By using time exposures that are minutes in length, star trails will result as the earth rotates. Figure 10 - 4 is such an example, with the added bonus of a full moon rising and illuminating the building. This exposure was 4.5 minutes in length at f/7.1, with ISO set to 400. Focal length was 24mm and the sensor was APS-C size.

Of course, this shot was taken in Manual mode with the shutter speed set to BULB. It is recommended that you also manually focus by switching the lens from AF to MF and rotating the focus barrel on the lens. An aperture of f/7.1 was chosen as a tradeoff between reasonable depth of field and long exposure times.

Because 24mm focal length is slightly wide angle for an APS-C sensor, the depth of field is increased over using a normal focal length (see Normal on page 33). According to depth of field tables, with these settings I only needed to focus at 14 feet to keep everything from 8 feet to infinity in focus (see Shifting the Depth of Field with Focus (Hyperfocal Distance) on page 24). Since I was more than 8 feet from the building, everything of interest in the shot (building and stars) was in focus.

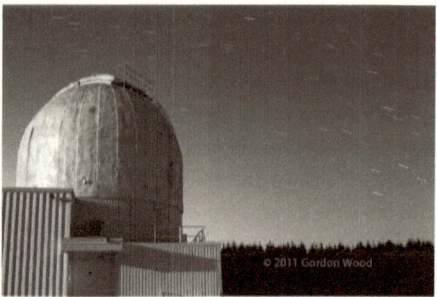

Figure 10 - 4 Moonlit Observatory and Star Trails

Photographic Exercise 7

It's time to work in the dark! The best way to do this exercise is to have a willing model. Find a location with a distant background with lights in it, such as a downtown park with buildings in the background or a back yard with garden lights. First, ensure you are not using Auto ISO. Instead, set it to 200.

1. Set the camera on a tripod and frame up the background. Remember to apply the Rule of Thirds, even at night. Decide where in the foreground you are going to place your subject. Also, ensure image stabilization on your lens is switched off, or you may get some very blurry images.

2. Set the exposure mode to Aperture Priority (A or Av) and choose something in the range of f/3.5 to f/5.6. Pop up the camera's flash using the button with the lightning bolt symbol, or attach an

accessory flash and set it to TTL or ETTL (you may have to refer to its manual to determine how to do this). Place your subject and take a shot.

3. Go into the camera's menu and find Flash Exposure Compensation (not Exposure Compensation) - see Using Flash Exposure Compensation to Balance Light on page 49. Adjust it down (-) by 1 complete stop and set this change. Now repeat the shot you just took. Reset the Flash Exposure Compensation to zero before doing the next step.

4. Now switch to Program mode (P) and take the same shot.

Analysis:

In Aperture Priority mode, you may have noticed that the shutter stayed open for several seconds. This is because the camera is trying to expose the entire scene properly without the contribution of the flash. When the flash fires, it gives off enough light to illuminate your subject but not much, if any, of the background.

By applying Flash Exposure Compensation to the second shot, you were reducing the amount of flash output, but not affecting the background exposure. You should notice that your subject was not as brightly lit in the second shot. In this way, you can use Flash Exposure Compensation to control the balance between background and foreground.

In Program mode, the opposite is true. The camera's exposure is completely determined by the amount of light that the flash is able to illuminate the scene and your subject with. Since flash duration is very short, the shutter only needs to stay open for a fraction of a second.

The end result is that Aperture (or Shutter) Priority mode gives you a better balanced photo at night by attempting to expose both background and subject in a balanced way. In Program mode, you only see what the flash can illuminate.

Photographic Exercise 8

For this one, you'll have to wait for a clear night and definitely use a tripod and shutter release. Use a fixed ISO (try 200) and a relatively wide focal length (ie. less than 35mm). See if you can find the North Star (Polaris). Aim the camera so that it is approximately centered on it. If not, any part of the sky will do.

1. Set the camera to Manual Mode. Use the controls to set the shutter speed to BULB and the aperture to about f/8. Some cameras have two Command Wheels which allow the shutter speed and aperture to be set separately. Some use the front Command Wheel and the rear panel joystick/control wheel to set them separately. Others require you to change the shutter speed with the Command Wheel and the aperture by holding down the Exposure Compensation button and turning the Command Wheel at the same time.
    BULB can be found by adjusting the shutter speed toward the slower values, and is the next one after the 30 second (30") value.

2. Go into the camera's menu and ensure that Long Exposure Noise Reduction is **OFF.**

3. Manually focus at infinity so that the stars are sharp in the viewfinder. Press and lock the shutter release. Do not bump the tripod during exposure. The camera may display the elapsed time on its LCD screen, but if not, time out a 2 minute exposure and release the shutter.
4. Now, switch **ON** the Long Exposure Noise Reduction function. Take another 2 minute exposure. Note that it may take 2 minutes for the camera to process the image after you take the shot.
    Note: If the stars are dim in the final images, try 3 minute and 4 minute exposures.

Analysis:
The first shot you took may show some short star trails that appear to circle around the North Star. But you may also see other bright objects that are clearly not stars. These are caused by noise in the sensor system. In the second shot, you should see a much clearer set of star trails because Long Exposure Noise Reduction subtracts out the noise from the sensor (although you have to wait longer for it to process the image).

Notice in the longer exposures at 3 or 4 minutes that the trails are brighter, and longer due to the rotation of the earth.

CHAPTER 11: PANORAMICS

Let's start by defining a panoramic. If you were to take a series of images in rapid succession by rotating your torso as you shot, you could assemble an extra-wide picture by overlapping the images. This action is commonly referred to as panning.

With panoramic software readily available today, we can let the program automatically 'stitch' the overlapping images together, rather than using scissors and tape. Some cameras have panoramic software built in and can perform this function without a computer. The software works by recognizing common features or details in each of the shots and determining how to connect successive images together at these points.

Notice that the word overlapping has already been used here twice. This is an important concept. Successful panoramics are made by providing enough overlap between successive shots so that the software can find these detail points and make the connections.

Equipment You'll Need

A tripod is strongly recommended because it will help you keep the horizon level as you pan, and provide you with a guide for the amount of overlap between shots.

If the tripod legs and/or the tripod head are not level throughout the panning range, the horizon will droop from one shot to another. The software will have to distort the individual shots in order to have them line up with each other. The end result is that you will have to crop the final image more than if the horizon was level in each shot.

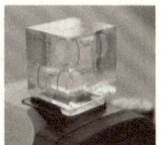

To avoid this, I have glued a bubble level to the base of my tripod legs, and also use a hot shoe bubble level (right) on the camera. I first get the legs as level as I can with the tripod bubble level, then pan the head while watching the hot shoe bubble level. If it varies, I will re-check that the legs are level then tweak the tripod head controls until there is little or no change throughout the panning range.

Yes - this sounds fiddly. You could forget the tripod and create a panoramic by stitching together handheld shots. This is a personal choice, but my preference is to always use a tripod to ensure I don't have to heavily crop the image after it's stitched.

Setting Focal Length

In Chapter 5: Lenses and Sensors, it was stated that focal lengths shorter than normal (ie. wide angle) produce bending of straight lines. If we use a short focal length, the panoramic software will have to distort each of the shots in order to make them line up for stitching. The more distortion, the more cropping of the final panoramic will be required.

For that reason, set the focal length (if using a zoom lens) to the normal focal length for the sensor type in your camera and leave it there for the entire sequence. Alternately, use a prime lens of normal focal length. This would be 30-33mm for an APS-C sensor and about 50mm for full frame.

Longer than normal focal lengths can be used without concern for 'barrel' or 'pincushion' distortion that short focal lengths produce. Keep in mind, however, that depth of field reduces as focal length is increased.

Choosing the Right Creative Mode

Imagine you're shooting a panoramic made up of photos that have dramatically different light content. In any mode but Manual, each photo would be exposed differently because the light metering system built into your camera tries to set the exposure automatically to an average 18% grey level. In this scenario, the panoramic wouldn't look right because the inherently darker scenes would be forced to look lighter compared to the others, resulting in a patchy-looking result.

Certainly, you could try matching the exposures in software before stitching, but it's easier to get it right in the camera. In Manual mode, I pan the entire scene first, using the camera's bar graph meter to set a shutter speed/aperture combination that *averages* a normal exposure. As a result, some shots will be slightly over-exposed and others under. As long as the histograms for all photos don't show any clipping at the black or white points, they're acceptable.

> **STARTING TIP:** Since panoramics tend to be of landscapes, choose an aperture value in the range f/16 to f/22 to maximize depth of field. Since you're using a tripod, don't worry if the shutter speed you have to use for proper exposure is less than 1/30th of a second (particularly in low light) since the tripod should eliminate blur due to camera shake. If you have a depth of field calculator available, manually focus to the hyperfocal distance to ensure the horizon is in focus too.

Choose an ISO Value

 The ISO value you use is at your discretion, but ensure that you use a fixed ISO setting rather than Auto ISO. If ISO changes while you are shooting your sequence, some shots may be brighter than others if the camera's metering system reads a significant variation in light across the scene.

Setting White Balance

 Similar to the argument in the last two topics, you don't want the camera to change the color balance as you pan because of changing content. Choose one of the presets instead of Auto. For instance, if shooting on an overcast day, use the Cloudy Bright setting. If shooting an indoor scene under fluorescent lights, use the Fluorescent setting. If you have access to a photo editing program that allows white balance adjustment, don't worry about what preset you choose, because you can correct all the shots by the same amount if the preset you chose results in wonky color.

Taking Control of Focus

Most DSLR lenses have a switch allowing you to disengage the motor that automatically focuses your lens before you take a shot. For panoramics, set it to manual focus (MF). The reason for this is that as you pan to take each of the shots, the camera may refocus on something close in or far away, especially if there's an object in one of the shots that is prominent. That could result in uneven focus across the panoramic. Pick one focus setting that works for the whole panoramic and leave it there.

Taking the Shots

Decide on Number of Shots and Orientation

There is a tendency to take a large number of shots when shooting panoramics because we think the result will be impressive. Unless your goal is to wrap an entire room with a panoramic, less is actually more. Consider this - the more shots you stitch together, the skinnier the panoramic will be, to the point of looking ridiculous. My personal preference is to limit the number of shots to 2, 3 or 4 at the most in the final version. See an example sequence in Figure 11 - 1. I may shoot 6 to 8 shots on location, but that gives me the opportunity to pick the best handful to merge into a panoramic.

To ensure that sufficient overlap is provided between shots, I strive for 25%. If there's any doubt about the software's ability to join the images, a generous overlap should reduce concerns. If I'm panning from left to right, this means I want the rightmost 25% of my first shot to be the same as the leftmost 25% of my second shot, and so on. Overlaps less than 25% will certainly work, but do some trials with your software to see what you can get away with.

Remember that there will be a difference in the number of degrees of rotation of the tripod head to achieve 25% between landscape (horizontal) and portrait (vertical) camera orientation. On the base of my tripod head, I have marked intervals for each orientation, so that I don't need to judge 25% overlap through the viewfinder as I pan.

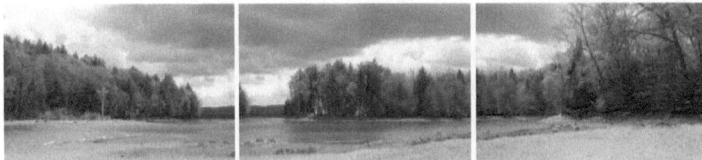

Figure 11 - 1 Raw Panoramic Shot Sequence

Shoot Rapidly

Light changes and clouds move and change shape over time. Rapid shooting of your sequence is recommended. That's where the interval marks on the tripod head will help. Simply shoot, rotate the head to the next mark, shoot again, and so on.

Finally, try to avoid shooting on windy days. The software will have difficulty stitching together foliage that's in a different position in successive shots as it flails in the wind.

Stitching the Images Together

I am not going to make any specific recommendations for panoramic software in this book. I will say, in my humble opinion, that the best software for this task came free and bundled with a point-and-shoot camera I purchased. I found that a certain high end photo editing package (that shall remain nameless) had a horrible, overly complex panoramic function that was slow, gave too many processing choices, and generally created contorted panoramics that needed an inordinate amount of cropping.

Figure 11 - 2 shows a result using my favorite software. Notice that the horizon is straight. Another program produced a curved horizon for the same panoramic, which is clearly unacceptable. The other feature of this final image is that very little cropping is required because the software did only minimal twisting of the images to match them up.

To find panoramic software, the best approach may be to do an online search and try some low cost alternatives, unless you've already sunk money into that expensive photo editing package. If you have, there is always the option of purchasing third party plug-ins that usually provide better control over the final image than the software they plug into.

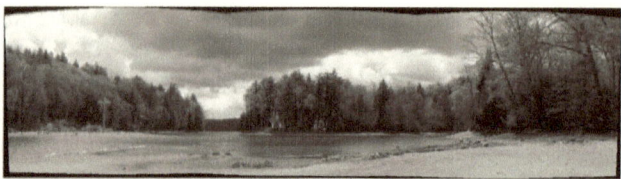

Figure 11 - 2 Stitched but Uncropped Panoramic

Photographic Exercise 9

In this exercise, find a location that will give you interesting subject matter that would benefit from being photographed in panoramic. Examples are boats in a marina or a distant city skyline. This may seem like a fussy setup (and it is), but it will give you superior control over the end result.

1. Set up your tripod and ensure that the legs and head are level. Pan the camera through the range you intend to photograph and ensure that the hot shoe bubble level does not change very much. If it does, check again that the legs and head are properly levelled.
2. Switch the lens to Manual Focus and focus on the most important feature of your panoramic.
3. Set the lens to 'normal' focal length (30-33mm for APS-C) or use a prime lens of, or close to, normal focal length.
4. Set the White Balance to a preset other than Auto White Balance.
5. Determine how many shots will make up your panoramic and what you want to include from the scene in front of you. Also determine whether you'll shoot in landscape (horizontal) orientation or portrait (vertical) orientation. You might choose portrait if you have tall buildings or trees

that you want to capture in their entirety. Once a choice is made, pan through your intended panoramic and determine the intervals at which you should stop for each shot such that about 25% overlap between adjacent shots is achieved. You might want to put tape marks on the tripod head so that you can take the shots rapidly without guessing. Note that this interval will change depending on the orientation and focal length.

6. Use Manual mode, push the shutter button halfway and roughly get an idea of what to set shutter speed and aperture to, using the camera's meter scale. For landscapes, you may want to set the aperture to as high an f/ number as possible to maximize depth of field. Pan the camera through the entire panoramic range and determine an average exposure and set the shutter speed and aperture to that.

7. Take the shots rapidly one after the other, using the interval marks on the tripod as your overlap guide. Play back the images and check their histograms to ensure no shots are either excessively over- or under-exposed. Adjust exposure as necessary and re-shoot the sequence.

8. When finished, remember to return White Balance to Auto.

Analysis:
This process can be very manual and take some time to perform, but using manual settings will ensure that the camera's white balance, focus and exposure will stay constant as you pan and shoot. Otherwise, the stitched image will never look right.

Choosing a 'normal' focal length is also important because wide angle focal length may produce curved lines in the scene. This makes it harder to stitch the images together, resulting in more cropping of the stitched image.

Don't worry - this becomes easier with practice, and the results are worth the hassle!

NOTES:

CHAPTER 12: HIGH DYNAMIC RANGE (HDR)

A relative newcomer to the world of digital photography is HDR. Thanks to today's computing power, this function broadens the creative spectrum for photographers.

Let's imagine you're photographing the interior of a cathedral on a sunny day. Depending upon how your camera's metering system is reading the light in the scene, you may either get:

- properly exposed stained glass windows but a very dark nave with no shadow detail, or
- a properly exposed nave but stained glass windows with all detail blown out due to the sun coming through them, or
- a reasonably average overall exposure but no shadow detail in the nave, and little or no highlight detail in the stained-glass windows

Why does this happen? With our naked eye, we can see all shadow and highlight detail at the same time, but the camera doesn't seem to be recording it.

As you may recall from Chapter 2: Exposure on page 9, the DSLR's sensor is limited to recording 256 levels of grey (brightness) between the darkest black and the brightest white. This is its *dynamic range*.

High Dynamic Range (HDR) processing is performed in software. It works by combining three separate images, one of which is intentionally underexposed, a normally exposed version and a third that is intentionally overexposed. All three must be fairly well aligned, but to an extent, the software can align them before processing. More than three images can actually be used, but for the discussion here, three will be assumed.

By taking highlight detail from the underexposed image, shadow detail from the overexposed image and mid-brightness detail from the normally exposed image, an image that contains all of this detail is produced. High dynamic range implies that the resultant image exceeds the 256-level capability of the camera sensor.

This capability is also available on some cameras, but generally using only two images: one underexposed and one overexposed. Further, output in this format is only available in JPEG, not RAW.

The reason that an underexposed image can capture more highlight detail than a normally exposed image is that underexposing shifts the histogram to the left, leaving more room at the right end to accommodate highlights. Likewise, overexposing leaves more room at the left end of the histogram to record shadow detail. In a sense, we're using the limited dynamic range of the sensor to capture only what we need in each image. This is illustrated in Figure 12 - 1.

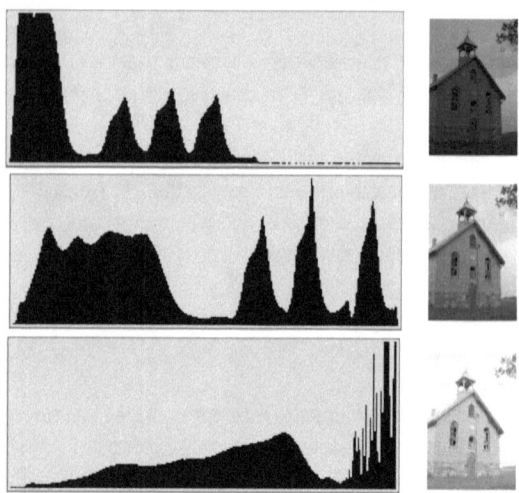

Figure 12 - 1 Under-, Normal and Overexposed Histograms for HDR

Equipment You'll Need

Although not as important as it was for panoramics, a tripod will help ensure that all three of your exposures are aligned with each other.

If your camera is not capable of *processing* HDR images internally, software for your computer will also be required. Note that all DSLR's are capable of producing the three images, so a built-in HDR function is not a necessity.

Ideal Conditions

Interiors make ideal subjects because everything remains stationary while you take the sequence of three exposures. If someone walks through the scene during the sequence, however, it can cause artifacts in the final HDR merge.

If working outdoors with flagpoles or vegetation in the scene, wait for a calm moment with no breeze. If photographing a water scene, bobbing boats will likewise create artifacts. For these reasons, evening may be the best time to work. You will also get the added benefit of Magic Hour light.

Using Manual Focus

Because auto focus may choose a different item to focus on as the exposure changes in the shot sequence, a good practice is to switch the lens to manual focus (MF) and focus once on an important part of the scene.

Setting White Balance

Similarly, white balance could change during the three exposures if the camera is left in Auto White Balance mode. Choose a preset instead that best matches the light you are working in.

Using Auto Exposure Bracketing (AEB)

The easiest and quickest way to set up your camera for an HDR shot is to use auto exposure bracketing. You may have to crack open your camera's manual again to find out how to adjust it, but chances are you will be able to find it in your camera's menu.

 To my surprise, however, some DSLRs do not provide this function. If yours falls into this category, you will have to use Exposure Compensation (page 18) to take your under- and overexposed shots. Use the same number of (-) stops for the underexposed shot as you do for the (+) stops for the overexposed shot.

Once into the AEB menu item, you may see either a bar graph or a selection of aperture increments (in stops). If you turn the Command Wheel, you will see two bars on the graph move apart by the number of stops that you require. These are the under- and overexposure amounts. A third bar at zero (assuming you haven't also used Exposure Compensation) represents the normal exposure. On other cameras, you simply select the amount of under- and overexposure you want. Press the SET or OK button to confirm these choices.

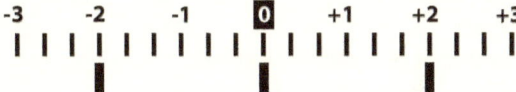

Note that AEB and Exposure Compensation settings will be active as long as the camera is powered up. When the camera is switched off then on again, however, the AEB settings will probably disappear but the Exposure Compensation settings will not. Be sure to zero out these settings if you no longer need them!

Choosing a Creative Mode

In most cases, depth of field is important in HDR images. In this case, you would choose Aperture Priority and use a small aperture (high f/number). AEB settings will be active in all Creative Modes except for Manual, so you can also use Shutter Priority or Program if you wish.

With AEB settings dialed in, you simply take three shots in a row. The same sequence can be repeated as many times as desired. If using Exposure Compensation instead to create the three exposures, you will have to adjust the exposure manually each time to get the underexposed, normal and overexposed images.

Merging the Exposures

Creating merged images on a computer is preferred over the built-in HDR feature available on a few cameras. A sequence of more than two or three images can be used in most software and you have more control over the result.

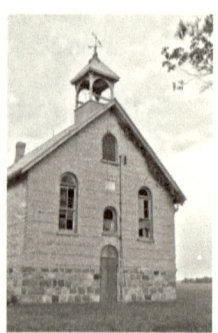

Various effects can be created during the merge, ranging from a natural result through to a very surrealistic one. HDR software provides you with control over the end effect with a number of preset choices and slider controls for the final tweak.

Photographic Exercise 10

Find a location that presents a wide range of lighting conditions in one photograph. Examples are a dark church interior combined with bright light coming through stained glass windows, or a sunset on the horizon with a field in shadow in the foreground. Best results are obtained when there is no motion (ie. wind blowing trees).

1. Mount the camera to a tripod to ensure that all shots making up the HDR image are perfectly aligned.
2. Choose an exposure mode you would prefer to work in (Program, Aperture Priority or Shutter Priority – it doesn't matter which).
3. Go into the camera's menu and find Auto Exposure Bracketing (AEB). Dial in +2 stops. You may have to reference your manual for this. Alternately, take 3 shots in a row using Exposure Compensation to produce one shot that is 2 stops underexposed, one shot that is normally exposed and one shot that is 2 stops overexposed.
4. You can use Auto Focus (AF) if you wish, but you might choose to set your lens to Manual Focus (MF) in case the camera tends to refocus between shots. Rapidly fire off the 3 shots. Play them back and you'll see from the histograms how the exposure has changed between all three shots. These are now ready to be combined in HDR software.

REMINDER: Don't forget to zero your AEB or Exposure Compensation settings when you are finished.

QUICK SOLUTION GUIDE

To summarize what you've learned, and to help you get results faster, consult the tables below:

Desired Result	Setup Required
Portrait with soft background	Use the widest aperture possible. The best lens is a prime lens because they have the best maximum aperture capability (lowest f/number). Use a slight telephoto focal length to compress depth of field even further. Separate your subject from the background as much as possible.
Night portrait with lights in background forming large blurry circles (bokeh)	As above, if available, use a fast prime lens at maximum aperture. A telephoto prime (or zoom if not available) works even better for softening background. Mount the camera on a tripod. Use Aperture Priority or Shutter Priority to ensure the background is properly exposed and pop up the built-in flash. Manually focusing on the subject may be necessary.
Daytime outdoor portrait	Use Program mode along with a flash (built-in or accessory) to fill in harsh shadows). Use a softbox on the flash if available. Alternately, use a golden reflector to bounce sunlight onto the subject.
Landscapes with sharp detail from close-in out to the horizon	Use a small aperture (f/16 to f/22). A wide angle lens will also increase the depth of field and make a more dramatic capture. Focus manually at a point that will just bring the horizon into sharp focus - no further (hyperfocal distance). Check dofmaster.com or get a depth of field calculator for your smartphone to determine hyperfocal distance.
Travel photos with dramatic color and contrast	Use a polarizing filter to make white clouds pop against a blue sky. Try to shoot at 'magic hour' as much as possible to get longer dramatic shadows and warm, intense colors.
Night photo of an approaching car where the headlight 'trails' are in front of it. Alternately, a night photo of a receding car with tail light trails behind the car.	Mount the camera on a tripod. Check the camera menu and ensure flash is set for First Curtain Sync. Use Aperture Priority or Shutter Priority. Pop up the built-in flash and press the shutter while the car is still some distance away (but close enough that the flash will illuminate it). For trailing tail lights, set camera for Second Curtain Sync and press the shutter just before the tail lights come into the frame.
Long time exposure of star trails (usually several minutes).	Mount the camera on a tripod and use a remote shutter release. Set Long Exposure Noise Reduction to ON. Manually focus on the stars and use a normal focal length. Dial in Manual mode and set shutter speed to BULB. Set aperture to about f/8 for shorter exposures or f/22 for very long ones. Lock the remote release during exposure to avoid jarring the camera.

Problem	Solution
Portrait with bright background results in dark subject	Try using Spot metering and centering the viewfinder on the subject's face. Alternately, intentionally increase exposure by using positive (+) Exposure Compensation.
Color cast in all shots. White looks either bluish or orange-yellow	White balance is not correct. First check that you are set to Auto White Balance. If so, the camera may be getting fooled by mixed light sources (ie. daylight from window and incandescent lamps indoors). If not, ensure that you're not using a white balance preset that's not suited to the light you are shooting in. For example, an Incandescent preset will produce a very blue cast on outdoor shots.
Winter or white beach sand landscapes look dark	If the camera's metering system reads mostly the light reflected from a bright surface, it will reduce the exposure until it averages a mid-grey. Snow looks grey rather than white. In such scenes, use 1 to 2 stops of positive (+) Exposure Compensation to make white look white.
Sky looks normally exposed, but foreground is dark and without detail. Sometimes it's the reverse - washed out sky but foreground is properly exposed.	The camera's sensor has a limited dynamic range that it can record, so we have to help it out a bit. A graduated filter can be used to darken the sky while not affecting the foreground.
Lens either focuses on the wrong thing, or hunts around for something to focus on when the light gets dim.	Auto focus can get fooled. Most lenses have a switch labelled AF/MF. In this case, switch to MF (Manual Focus) and rotate the focus ring on the lens (not the zoom ring) and focus on your subject.
Fast-moving subjects (athletes, race cars, pets or children) are always blurry	If focus is not the problem, shutter speed is too slow. Go into Shutter Priority and select as high a shutter speed as the light will allow (the camera will often flash the aperture value or display Low Light in this case). If ISO is set to Auto, manually select a higher ISO value, which will allow you to increase shutter speed further. Be aware that high ISO=increasing noise on the image.
Panoramic shots refuse to 'stitch' properly together in software. Others stitch OK but require a lot of cropping.	If you don't provide sufficient overlap between shots in your sequence, there may not be enough information for the program to join the shots. Also, shots that lack detail (such as soft cirrus clouds) present the same problem. The software needs distinct features or edges to match up shots. If all shots were made without a level tripod, the result may be a rounded horizon and a lot of unuseable area that has to be cropped from the edges.

GLOSSARY OF TERMS

AEB (Auto Exposure Bracketing) A setting that allows 3 exposures to be taken in a row: one underexposed, one normally exposed and one overexposed. The amount of under- and over-exposure can be set by the user. Used for HDR photography or to provide more than one exposure in case the normal exposure is not accurate.

AF (Auto Focus) A function in which the camera controls the focus motor in the lens until focus is achieved on a particular feature in the scene. Auto focus zones can be selected by the user, either individually or by the entire group.

Aperture A set of blades within the lens that form a variable opening. The size of the opening determines the amount of light that enters the camera. It also affects depth of field. This is analogous to the iris in the eye.

Aperture Priority A semi-automatic exposure mode in the camera. User selects a specific aperture and the camera sets the shutter speed, based on the amount of available light. Aperture remains fixed until changed.

APS-C A specific sensor size found largely in consumer DSLRs. Exact size may vary from manufacturer to manufacturer.

Auto Mode A setting in which aperture, shutter speed, ISO and built-in flash on/off are automatically determined by the camera. User cannot alter any of these parameters.

AWB (Auto White Balance) A setting in which the camera reads the color temperature of the light in the scene and automatically determines sensitivity weightings between the red, green and blue channels to make white look white in the recorded file.

Body (camera) The main part of the DSLR, to which a variety of lenses can be attached.

BULB A shutter speed setting in which the shutter will stay open as long as the shutter button is pressed.

Bokeh The formation of large petal-like shapes formed by out of focus elements in an image. The shape is usually created by the aperture blades and typically occurs when shallow depth of field (very wide apertures) is used.

Center Weighted Metering A form of light measurement in the camera in which only the light in the middle 65% to 75% of the viewfinder is used to determine exposure.

Color Temperature Measured in °K, this indicates the color balance of the light. Higher values imply strong blue content (ie. outdoors) while lower values tend toward red (ie. incandescent lamps).

Compressed Files A means of recording image information in which file size is reduced by deleting part of the data that is not absolutely needed ('lossy' compression). An example is the JPEG file type.

Creative Modes Exposure modes on the camera that give the user more control than Auto mode or other exposure presets. These include Program (P), Aperture Priority (Av or A), Shutter Priority (Tv or S) and Manual (M) modes.

Crop Factor The ratio of image area captured by a full frame sensor to the image area captured by a smaller sensor (ie. APS-C) when using a lens of the same focal length.

Custom White Balance A setting that allows the user to create a white balance preset based on a specific lighting setup. Most commonly used in studio settings where lighting color temperature is constant.

Depth of Field The range, in distance from the camera, over which the image is considered acceptably sharp. Numerically, it is the difference between the near focus limit and the far focus limit.

Depth of Field Preview A button on the camera that closes the lens aperture to the selected value (by either the user or the camera, depending on exposure mode) before taking the picture. This allows depth of field at that aperture to be evaluated visually in the viewfinder before taking the shot.

Diffuser Generally a fabric that softens a direct light source (ie. sun, flash) to make shadows less distinct.

DSLR (Digital Single Lens Reflex) A camera that uses interchangeable lenses and records the image using a digital sensor rather than film. Reflex refers to the fact that the user can preview the image in an optical viewfinder. The image from the lens is reflected by a mirror that flips up during picture taking. A pentaprism corrects the image reflected by the mirror so that the viewfinder image is properly oriented.

Dynamic Range In the context of a camera sensor, this is the maximum range of light intensity that can be recorded, from the darkest shadow detail to the brightest highlights.

ETTL (Evaluative Through The Lens) A means by which the camera reads ('meters') the light in a scene, in which several sensor zones and a computer algorithm are used to determine optimal exposure. Because it is measuring light passing through the lens, it takes into account light reduction caused by filters attached to the lens.

Evaluative Metering Canon's method of using ETTL to determine exposure.

Exposure The amount of light recorded by the sensor, determined by aperture, shutter speed and ISO.

Exposure Compensation The ability to increase or decrease exposure by a specific number of stops set by the user. The increase or decrease is applied to the normal exposure determined by the camera's metering system.

f/stop A number that expresses the lens aperture value, or size. Larger f/numbers relate to smaller apertures and smaller f/numbers relate to larger apertures. Small apertures provide greater depth of field but let less light into the camera.

First Curtain Sync A setting in which the flash fires at the beginning of the shutter opening sequence.

Flash Exposure Compensation A setting in which flash output can be increased or decreased over that which is determined by the camera. This is independent of camera exposure settings, and can be used to balance the background exposure with areas of the scene illuminated by the flash.

Focal Length The distance from the convergence point in a lens to the sensor plane. The longer the focal length, the closer the subject appears in the viewfinder and the recorded image. Measured in millimeters.

FP High Speed Sync A setting in the flash that allows the camera and flash to be used together at higher than the normal shutter speed limit for proper synchronization. It does this by firing the flash in several lower intensity bursts while the shutter is open.

Full Frame Sensor A DSLR sensor that is equivalent in dimensions to a 35mm film frame (24x36mm).

Grey Scale The range of brightness that appears in a scene. An 8 bit sensor is capable of recording 256 different brightness or grey levels.

HDR (High Dynamic Range) A method of creating images that have a dynamic range greater than that of the digital sensor. This is accomplished by shooting three identical shots, except one is underexposed, one is overexposed and the third is normally exposed. These are combined in software to create the final image.

Histogram A graphical representation of the brightness content in an image from black on the left end to white on the right end. Provides a means of determining whether over- or underexposure have occurred if the graph is strongly shifted to the right or the left, respectively. A centered and balanced graph generally represents acceptable exposure.

Hyperfocal Distance For a given f/stop, focal length and sensor size, this is the distance to which the lens should be focused to ensure that the image will be in focus from in front of the subject out to infinity.

Image Circle The diameter of the circular image projected by a lens onto the back of the camera. Note that two lenses of the same focal length but designed for different sensor sizes will not have the same image circle diameter.

Image Stabilized Lens A lens with an internal element that is moved by servo motors in the horizontal and vertical directions. This movement counteracts movement created by the user when a tripod or other support is not used. This allows slower shutter speeds to be used while avoiding motion blur normally introduced at such speeds when hand holding the camera.

ISO In DSLRs, this setting determines the sensitivity of the sensor to light. Doubling the ISO setting is equivalent to increasing exposure by one stop. ISO values in sensors are equivalent to ISO values in film.

JPEG (Joint Photographic Experts Group) An image file format that uses lossy compression to reduce its stored size. Most DSLRs are set at the factory to record in this format by default.

Live View An alternative to using the optical viewfinder to preview the scene before taking the picture. It works by flipping up the mirror and using the sensor to display live video on the LCD panel.

Long Exposure Noise Reduction A camera custom function that reduces the noise, or random bright spots, in images made with shutter speeds longer than about one second.

Macro Refers to close up photography, but in strict terms means that the photographed subject is recorded as actual size (1:1) on the sensor. Special lenses are required to achieve this.

Magic Hour The hour around sunrise or sunset. Color temperature is lower at these times and the light is a warm red-orange. Color is more saturated than at mid-day and shadows are longer, leading to more dramatic shots. Car commercials tend to be shot at magic hour.

Manual An exposure mode in which there is no automatic exposure setting by the camera. The photographer takes complete control by setting both the aperture and shutter speed manually.

Matrix Metering Nikon's method for determining exposure by measuring light in several zones across the scene and creating an exposure in which the brightness of the image averages to an 18% grey (mid grey). Similar to Canon's Evaluative Metering method.

NEF Nikon's uncompressed image file format. Similar to RAW file format.

Neutral Density Filter A filter used in front of the lens to intentionally reduce the light entering the lens. The term neutral refers to the fact that this filter does not introduce a color hue.

Panoramic A single image comprised of two or more individual camera images joined seamlessly together. Implemented in software.

Partial Metering A form of light measurement in the camera in which only the light in the middle 5% to 10% of the viewfinder is used to determine exposure.

Pixel The smallest picture element that can be recorded by the sensor.

Polarizing Filter A filter used in front of the lens to increase contrast against blue skies and reduce glare on water surfaces.

Prime Lens A lens with a fixed focal length. This type of lens provides better maximum apertures (lower f/number) than zoom lenses. This is a lens of choice for portrait photographers because of the shallow depth of field it creates at maximum aperture.

Program An exposure mode in which the camera automatically sets both aperture and shutter speed. Similar to Auto except it does not set ISO value or force the built-in flash on in low light situations.

Program Shift A means by which the aperture/shutter speed combination set by the camera in Program mode can be changed if desired.

RAW Similar to NEF files, these are uncompressed files. Storage space is larger than for JPEG files, but they are preferred when considerable editing will be performed on the image file

Resolution The total number of pixels that a sensor can record. This is typically expressed in megapixels, or millions of pixels. Resolution can also apply to the printed page, where it is expressed as dots per inch (dpi) or pixels per inch (ppi).

Rule of Thirds A composition guideline for landscape photographs in which the horizon is placed at either one-third of the distance from the bottom of the frame or one-third of the distance from the top of the frame. It can also be applied to placing a subject between the left and right edges of the frame.

Second Curtain Sync A setting in which the flash fires at the end of the shutter opening sequence.

Shutter Priority A semi-automatic exposure mode in the camera. User selects a specific shutter speed and the camera sets the aperture, based on the amount of available light. Shutter speed remains fixed until changed.

Spot Metering A form of light measurement in the camera in which only the light in the middle 1% to 5% of the viewfinder is used to determine exposure.

Stop A term which is used to express the equivalent of either a change in aperture by one f/stop, or a doubling or halving of shutter speed. One stop is a change in light intensity or exposure by a factor of two.

TTL (Through The Lens) A means by which the camera reads ('meters') the light in a scene. Because it is measuring light passing through the lens, it takes into account light reduction caused by filters attached to the lens. Similar to ETTL except it is not necessarily using a multi-zone algorithm to determine exposure.

UV Filter A filter used in front of the lens to reduce daytime haziness introduced by ultraviolet light. This effect is less pronounced in DSLRs than for film cameras, so they are often installed merely to protect the lens against scratches.

White Balance Refers to the equalization of output levels between the red, green and blue channels in a recorded image file when photographing a white or neutral grey surface. White balance presets in the camera adjust the balance between channels to correct for color temperature of specific light sources.

NOTES:

INDEX

Numerics

A

B

C

www.ingramcontent.com/pod-product-compliance
Lightning Source LLC
Chambersburg PA
CBHW022115170526
45157CB00004B/1643